MW01680450

Seeking Spiritual Clarity: the Murky Perspective of Evil

Seeking Spiritual Clarity: The Murky Perspective of Evil

by Don Umphrey

Quarry Press • P.O. Box 181736 • Dallas, TX 75218
quarrypress@msn.com • www.quarrypressbooks.com

Copy Editor: Susie Meyer
Cover design and layout: Angie Maddox
Cover photo: © Bart Sadowski - istockphoto.com

Published by Quarry Press, Dallas, TX.

Printed in the United States of America.

ISBN: 978-0-9714958-8-3

Library of Congress Control Number: 2008938699

Dedicated to my wife, Kim,

with gratitude for her love and support.

CONTENTS

Chapter One:

The True Source of Evil

November 6, 1973, is a day that lives in infamy for me. In the wee hours of the morning, I had called the suicide prevention center in a state of near hysteria and started to spill out my story. "Are you drinking?" a female voice inquired.

"Of course."

"You need to stop."

I slammed down the phone, a fitting response to an irrational woman. Here I was facing the horror of growing insanity, and she told me to cease the only activity that brought me any relief.

I dozed for a little while and then awakened with a driving certainty of impending doom. I chugged a beer. No help. I turned to a second and third … Reinforcements still needed … Fifth, sixth … eighth … .

My mind reeled out of control, so I turned to straight Scotch whiskey. Still no relief.

Despair seemed on the verge of totally consuming me. At the age of 27, total insanity or death appeared certain. I had not a clue of where to turn for help.

That was the worst day of my life, and as I write these words, it occurred nearly 35 years ago. Ironically, it also turned out to be the best day of my life. Like the lost son starving in a pig pen from Jesus' parable,[1] it marked the beginning of a new direction of seeking God to guide me in sobriety and every other facet of my life.

Heading away from the pig pen, the murky vision from my self-indulgent past started to clear. I came to see that my drinking life was characterized by increasing self-centeredness. Discussing this with some friends several years later, I was asked, "Where does Satan fit into this picture?"

I hadn't really thought of my descent into alcoholism in terms of being influenced by Satan. As the source of evil, however, who else but Satan would have served as the cheerleader for my walk away from God? Exploring this idea further, I have come to see that the devil's impact on me goes far beyond my near destruction from alcoholism.

What about you? What is the devil's influence on your life?

Have you bought into the devil's deception by thinking of his impact only in terms of huge, world-impacting events, such as the fall of humanity, the temptation of Jesus, and the battle of Armageddon?

Undoubtedly, you already have the big picture: Satan was successful in tempting Adam and Eve. As a result, we live in a fallen world and depend on the grace of Jesus for salvation. But how might Satan tempt you during your next shopping trip?

Many books have been written on spiritual warfare, demons, witchcraft, and exorcism. But what do these topics tell you about how the devil attempts to influence the way you talk to your co-workers, friends, and loved ones?

Jesus called Satan the "father of lies."[2] What lies are being whispered to you? Do you believe them? Is it possible that you do believe them and don't know it?

Perhaps Satan's goal is not to destroy you with a lion-like attack. His strategy for you might include a long series of smaller temptations likened to 100,000 mosquito bites over a period of time that would slowly sap your energy and finally cause you to scratch yourself to death.

These "mosquito bites" are the not the "black sins" but the seemingly more benign shortcomings of which Bible-believing Christians may be guilty, such as judging others, gossiping, or failing to live one day at a time.

The approach here is based on the tree-fruit relationship pointed out by Jesus. "No good tree bears bad fruit, nor does a bad tree bear good fruit. Each tree is recognized by its own fruit … ."[3]

We recognized this phenomenon even when we were children. For example, we would have had completely different thoughts about another child we observed torturing an animal compared to one helping a handicapped senior citizen.

As Christians, we've seen the tree-fruit connection in the words and actions of Jesus reflecting the fact that He is the Son of God.

We may use a similar analogy with Satan but in the opposite direction. The temptations you face reflect Satan's very nature as the origin and epitome of evil.

God, Himself, through His inspired word, is this volume's source of information about the characteristics of Satan. My perspective as the author is as an evangelical Christian who believes the Bible is God's inspired truth.

The Bible's view of Satan is often lost on today's culture. This is probably the result of Satan's lies; if people don't understand the devil, they have no idea about the ways he may attack them.

Views of the evil one:

Here are some false perspectives you may recognize and which may, to a greater or lesser degree, be a part of your belief system.

(1) Satan is portrayed as a caricature or cartoon-like. His very existence is acknowledged only by unsophisticated, superstitious individuals. This view dismisses Satan as a type of joke. The cartoon Satan bears no resemblance to the one "who leads the whole world astray."[4]

In The Screwtape Letters, C. S. Lewis writes as "Screwtape," a mid-management-level demon who gives advice to his nephew,

"Wormwood." The nephew is a novice demon assigned to lead a young man to hell. In regards to this false portrayal of Satan, Lewis writes the following as Screwtape:

> The fact that "devils" are predominantly comic figures in the modern imagination will help you. If any faint suspicion of your existence begins to arise in his mind, suggest to him a picture of something in red tights, and that since he cannot believe in that (it is an old textbook method of confusing them) he therefore cannot believe in you.[5]

(2) The opposite fictional depiction of the cartoon character shows Satan as a monster. Rather than Frankenstein's creation, the evil character is the devil. This villain takes possession of otherwise innocent people and makes them say and do horrible things (via Hollywood special effects, of course).

Who can ever forget the head-spinning, vile-talking, pea-soup-spitting 12-year-old girl depicted in the feature film *The Exorcist*?

Since most of us have never personally witnessed Satanic possession in these terms, this view doesn't ring true, either—at least for adults. The movie monster turns Satan into a different type of joke distantly removed from "the prince of this world,"[6] a description of Satan given by Jesus.

(3) Satan is a myth created long ago to account for man's evil. This "enlightened" perspective is based on a world view that denies any spiritual basis to life. It purports that the only real "truths" are

those that man can prove.

This view is evident when watching television programs featuring so-called experts who dismiss biblical accounts as folklore and allegories handed down from earlier civilizations.

(4) The devil is presented in terms of evil that affect only the worst of the worst, like Adolph Hitler. People then may point their fingers at the evil person and shake their heads in dismay while holding themselves unaccountable. This perspective fits perfectly in a society where individuals commonly avoid taking responsibility for their own actions.

(5) Satan may be acknowledged as a spiritual being of evil, but the extent of his power is called into question. Writing in *People of the Lie: The Hope for Healing Human Evil*, best-selling author M. Scott Peck said he was present at two exorcisms. Based on his observations, Peck concluded that Satan does not understand science. He writes,

> Science is an anti-narcissistic phenomenon. It assumes a profound human tendency to self-deception, employs the scientific method to counteract it, and holds truth higher than any personal desire.[7]

The scientific method to which this author refers is taught at the graduate level at every major university. Would Peck have us believe that Satan is not intelligent enough to earn a masters degree or Ph.D.?

While teaching at the university level, I used the scientific method to conduct academic research for more than a quarter century. I've observed that it is fallible on countless levels and that ego reigns supreme in academia. My guess is that Satan would want us to think he does not understand science.

Peck's observation about Satan's mentality is not based on any description found in the Bible. John wrote, "… the whole world is under the control of the evil one."[8] Could the world be controlled by Peck's version of Satan?

(6) Through Christian literature, many people have become familiar with spiritual warfare conducted in the invisible world inhabited by angels and demons. It may be interesting to speculate about these invisible battles, but excessive dwelling on such occurrences may lead us to overlook our own personal spiritual battles in the visible world.

(7) Finally, Bible-believing Christians know that Satan is the source of evil, but many do not have any idea about the actual mechanisms of temptation used by the devil or the change in an individual's perspective that follows succumbing to sin.

The purpose of this volume is to give you a true, biblically based description of the way the evil one attempts to influence our lives and its immediate and long-term effects.

Chapter 2 focuses on Satan's major motivation and how this is reflected in the temptations that you and I face. We know that by his actions in the Garden of Eden, the devil has already self-destructed, and this is also the fate of anyone who chooses to follow him. Self-destruction is the topic of Chapter 9.

The chapters in between, Chapters 3 through 8, describe characteristics of Satan and how they show up in the lives of individuals who already have yielded to temptation. We might think of these as steps along the road to self-destruction, but they are not all necessarily sequential. You will see that as these things occur, individuals become more like Satan and start perceiving the world in the same way that he does.

Of course, our goal is to become more like Jesus and to look at the world with ultimate clarity through His eyes. With this in mind, Chapter 10 describes the "moment of clarity" that precedes a person leaving the path to self-destruction and three different ways that one arrives at this moment. Chapter 11 details repentance and confession, further increments to leaving behind the old life in favor of salvation.

Chapter 12, which concludes this volume, summarizes the entire book by describing absolute pride (Satan's world view) in comparison to absolute humility (Jesus' world view) and the perspective of self that goes with each.

Please heed a gentle word of warning.

Jesus asked this question: "Why do you look at the speck of sawdust in your brother's eye and pay no attention to the plank in your own eye?"[9] In other words, it is much easier for me to find fault in someone else than to examine myself. But as long as I focus on someone else's faults, I don't have to do anything about my own. So, spiritually speaking, I stay exactly where I am instead of moving forward.

As you read the characteristics of Satan, it will be very easy for you to recognize these characteristics in someone else. You must consider them, however, in terms of the person you see in the mirror; otherwise, this book will do you more harm than good.

ENDNOTES: CHAPTER ONE

1. Luke 15: 11-32.
2. John 8: 44.
3. Luke 6: 43-44.
4. Revelation 12: 9.
5. C.S. Lewis, *The Screwtape Letters*, Harper-Collins, San Francisco, 2001, p. 32.
6. John 12: 31.
7. M. Scott Peck, *People of the Lie: The Hope for Healing Human Evil*, Touchstone, New York, 1983, pp. 208-209.
8. I John 5: 19.
9. Matthew 3: 7.

Questions for Self-Examination and Group Discussion: Chapter 1

1. Many people think of the devil as a myth. How would this belief affect one's life? Give examples of where and how the myth-idea is perpetuated.

2. What were your perceptions of the devil when you were a child? In terms of what you know now, were these thoughts accurate or inaccurate? Do your childhood perceptions of the evil one continue to influence your thoughts today? Why or why not?

3. Thinking about the things you've read about Satan in the Bible, what single thing stands out the most in your mind?

4. Name some ways you think Satan influenced the entire world during Bible times … During the last few centuries … During your lifetime.

5. This chapter lists seven ways that the devil may be perceived. With which of these do you most identify? Least identify? Can you think of ways not listed?

6. Name some specific ways that evil has influenced your life. (Saying that you are a sinner doesn't count. Be specific!) What is the greatest stumbling block in your life today?

7. When reading this book, how can you avoid the pitfall of focusing on the negative aspects in the lives of others instead of focusing on yourself?

Chapter Two:

Playing God

In high school, I thought I was the only guy with anxieties about girls. Some of my male classmates had it made—or so it looked to me. I'd see some of them walking down the hall holding hands with one of our school's most beautiful girls. Then a few weeks later, they would be escorting yet another foxy young lady.

I contrasted that to what was going on with me. I'd never had a "steady" girlfriend, and it took all the courage I could muster to call someone for a date. I was too self-conscious to dance fast, and when I took the girl home, I had a phobia about trying to kiss her goodnight. I was concerned I didn't know how to kiss right.

From my perspective, there were a bunch of Romeos at my high school and one big dud who looked back at me from the mirror.

That all changed after football season my senior year. I traded my spikes for a six-pack and started drinking beer on a regular basis.

I thought I'd discovered the world's greatest magic elixir. It immediately took away all my anxieties. It was as if I were a caterpillar emerging from a cocoon after 17 years.

As a fan of old movies, it seemed that a few brews transformed me into a combination of Errol Flynn and Fred Astair. In case you are not an old movie buff, Flynn's on-screen image was as a swashbuckler and lover, and Fred Astair was a great dancer.

I went away to college with the idea that alcohol was the solution to all of life's problems. Soon, I subscribed to a mantra that was popular at the time (late 1960s): "If it feels good, do it."

I also started viewing as old fogies the people at the church where I had grown up. I told my mother that Christianity would soon die because it lacked relevancy.

In retrospect, it is now clear to me that I had become Satan's disciple.

Am I being too harsh on myself? Not at all. Someone might say that I was a college boy doing some harmless experimentation with alcohol. In truth, however, I was guilty of idolatry and the self-exaltation that goes with it.

How does this make me a follower of Satan?

We'll come back to my part of this, but let's first examine Satan's role in this picture: His defining motivation is to be God and be worshipped accordingly.

Satan was originally an angel[1] but wasn't content with that lofty position. God quotes him as saying, "I will ascend to heaven; I will raise my throne above the stars of God . . . I will make myself like the Most High."[2]

Satan led a revolution against God[3] resulting in his expulsion from Heaven[4] along with one-third of the angels who were his followers.[5]

Who else but someone trying to be God would dare ask Jesus to bow down and worship him?[6]

In an apparent end-time prophecy, either Satan or one of his minions is called "the man of lawlessness" (who)

> will oppose and will exalt himself over everything that is called God or is worshipped, so that he sets himself up in God's temple, proclaiming himself to be God.[7]

From beginning to end, Satan is consistent in his desire to be God.

In the garden

Let's take a look at how this characteristic of Satan demonstrates itself repeatedly in the Garden of Eden.

Regarding the trees in the garden, here is what God had stated: "You are free to eat from any tree in the garden; but you must not eat from the tree of the knowledge of good and evil, for when you eat of it you will surely die."[8]

Sometime thereafter, Satan appeared as a serpent to Eve and asked her, "Did God really say, 'You must not eat from any tree in the garden'?"[9]

Compare the two quotations and answer the question for yourself.

If you answered "no," you got the correct answer. God did not say that. Satan attempted to twist God's words for his own purposes. Who else but a usurper would try to distort God's truth?

Eve answered Satan's question, and we will come back to this shortly. In the meantime, let's continue to look for signs of "playing God" in the words of the serpent.

"'You will not surely die,' the serpent said to the woman."[10] Here, the devil calls God a liar and claims to have more knowledge than God. Who else would say this except someone who thinks he is God?

Satan continued, "*For God knows* that when you eat of it your eyes will be opened.."[11] (emphasis mine) Only a God-pretender would dare venture to say what God knows.

Based on these scriptures, you can see that every time Satan opened his mouth, his defining motivation was glaringly obvious.

Recall the tree-fruit relationship discussed in the previous chapter. Satan's chief characteristic is reflected in the way he tempts people. This is obvious in his temptation to Eve "*You will be like God,* knowing good and evil."[12] (emphasis mine)

Eve's response

Now let's take a look at Eve's interaction with the devil.

Here's how Eve replied to Satan's question as to what God has really said, "We may eat fruit from the trees in the garden, but God did say, 'You must not eat fruit from the tree that is in the middle of the garden, and you must not touch it, or you will die.'"[13]

In replying to Satan, Eve both added to and subtracted from God's word, another form of playing God.

God had said, "You are free to eat."[14] Eve's response left out the idea of being "free." Then she added, "You must not touch it."[15] These changes appeared to make God "seem less generous and more demanding than he really was," according to Henry M. Morris.[16]

According to a principle found at the end of the New Testament, the penalty for adding to or subtracting from God's words are plagues and death, respectively.[17] By her actions that soon followed, Eve brought plagues and destruction on herself and everyone else. Simultaneously, she and Adam lost much of what God had promised in His first three recorded words to humanity, "You are free."[18]

As soon as Eve entered into a dialogue with Satan, she started seeing things the way he wanted her to see them, and her words portray God in a diminished position. She did not resist the devil[19] and kept on listening. Eve's perspective grew increasingly murky during this brief conversation with the source of evil. Her focus went from all of the trees in the garden to the only one that was taboo.

When Satan tempted her with the idea of being like God, Eve was fixated but was on the verge of making an important choice. Was she going to

- follow God's word or "play God" by doing what she thought was right?

- be content with what God had given her or strive for the "eye opening" experience?
- believe God or Satan?

By basing her decision on Satan's word, she let her vision supersede God's. In this way, she followed the devil and played God.

Where was Adam when all of this happened? Standing right beside Eve[20] like a proverbial bump on a log, letting all of this happen, and making himself a full partner in her decisions.

Looking at this in black and white, Eve's decision-making process seems ludicrous. God spoke the universe into existence and created everything in it, including humanity; He is everywhere, knows everything, and is timeless.

Surely Eve knew that God had made her from a rib taken from Adam's side and that God made Adam from dust. She already had enjoyed a personal relationship with her Creator. Weighing the choices makes Eve's decision a no-brainer. Right?

Answer this question: Have you ever done something you knew was not God's will in your life? If you answered yes, you did the same thing as Eve. You have played God.

As a result of their desire to "play God," Adam and Eve lost their eye-to-eye relationship with God, were banished from the perfect place He had created for them, and were subjected to the fallen world that we see around us, which includes pain and death.

We have inherited a murky view of the world, and it is hard to imagine having the 20-20 spiritual vision that was enjoyed by our first ancestors. Through Jesus Christ, we have the assurance of salvation and will be restored to a face-to-face relationship with God. Paul said it this way: "Now we see but a poor reflection as in a mirror; then we shall see face to face. Now I know in part; then I shall know fully, even as I am fully known."[21]

The "then" to which Paul refers is when we die. We then will see God face to face and will know fully because we no longer will live in a fallen world. We will be restored to the place God intended for us at the creation of the world.

In the meantime, though, we strive for as much clarity as possible and frequently make decisions similar to the one faced by Eve. Are we going to get Satan's murky perspective on things? Or are we going to accept our Creator's gift, his son Jesus Christ, and seek His perspective? It is only through Jesus that we can reclaim the freedom that was lost in the Garden of Eden.

How we "play" God

A desire to "play God," in one form or another, is at the root of every temptation you and I will ever face. This temptation is at odds with the First Commandment, "You shall have no other gods before me."[22] Jesus later restated this as the greatest commandment, "Love the Lord your God with all your heart and with all your soul and with all your mind."[23]

Surely, most of us never would actually attempt to take over for

God, would we? Certainly not as professed "Satan worshippers," but there are many ways those with the best of intentions end up "playing God."

When I was drinking and continually attempting to please myself, who was the sole arbiter of my ethics and morals? I was. While I never stated I wanted to take over for God, I "played God" by disregarding His will for my life and substituting my own. My actions cried out, "My will be done!"

I was also an idolater. Christians are told to take their anxieties to God.[24] When I had anxieties, where did I turn? Beer and booze. I put my faith in what I could purchase in clear, green and brown bottles.

Anything in one's life that supersedes the true God of the universe becomes that person's "god."

On this tendency Douglas J. Rumford wrote:

> Where is my trust, my confidence that my welfare is assured? … One of the basic tools of the evil one is to get us to bank on the wrong things. When we think there are quick answers to solve our security needs, we are sorely tempted. And he can attack us at a number of levels.[25]

We can identify Satan's work in our "attempt to bestow divine absoluteness on a finite object and spotlight it as the object of ultimate concern," according to Kerry Walters.[26]

A false god may be the thing we complain about the most or the first place on the receiving end of our time and resources.

Individuals involved with Internet pornography say they plan their days in order to spend solitary time with their computers. Others put their faith in their work. There are many other possibilities such as shopping, spending, eating, golfing, fishing, watching soap operas, and devotion to a sports team, to name only a few. Any person with an addictive behavior is an idolater.

It is no surprise, then, that the website of the Church of Satan contains the following statement of theology: "People have created Gods in many forms; pick one that might be useful to you."[27]

Beware, good causes—or even those we perceive as being righteous—have the potential to become our false gods. Suppose an individual makes a decision to work on behalf of environmental issues. With the passage of time, this may become a false god if this person's devotion to "the cause" exceeds the individual's devotion to God.

We could do the same thing with our devotion to either the Democratic or Republican Party, the women's movement, a service club, Boy Scouts, civil rights, support for missionaries, Little League, world peace—you name it. Surely, we would be attempting to put God in a box of our own making if we think of Him as the God of Pro-Life or any other cause, worthwhile or not.

Here is another way a false god might show up. A person does something really horrible that hurts others and brings reproach on him- or herself. Reports of these negative incidents sometimes are accompanied by a statement that the individual was "blinded by

____________.” Fill in the blank with greed, money, ambition, hatred, a desire for revenge — the list goes on. What happened here is that ___________ became number one in that person’s life, a false god. Guess who did the blinding?

Another way to play God is by attempting to do His job. Someone hurts us (ego-wise, socially, financially — the list goes on), and we want this person to suffer as a result. This type of sentiment flies in the face of the fact that paybacks are God’s job.[28]

Who ultimately will determine who will enter heaven? God, of course. But if based on the Bible as I interpret it, I think I can tell who will be saved and who will be excluded; that means I think my judgment is as good as God’s.

What about perfectionists? Only God can get it right every time.

People who never apologize for anything? They think they don’t have to apologize because they assume everything they do is right, the same as God.

Know-it-alls? This pretty much speaks for itself, doesn’t it?

“Playing God” may also deal with false perceptions of who has control. A young woman once told me that her anorexia was her attempt to exercise control in her life. Sometimes individuals who endeavor to control other people call it love, and they never would think about their efforts in terms of self-deification.

When we choose to rely on our own murky vision in this fallen world, we are on a course of self-destruction that affects the way we perceive ourselves and others—as you will see in the next chapter.

ENDNOTES: CHAPTER TWO

1. Ezekiel 28: 12-15.
2. Isaiah 14: 13-14.
3. Revelation 12: 7.
4. Isaiah 14: 12; Ezekiel 28: 16; Revelation 12: 8-9.
5. Revelation 12: 4.
6. Matthew 4:9.
7. II Thessalonians 2: 3-4.
8. Genesis 2: 16-17.
9. Genesis 3: 1.
10. Genesis 3: 4.
11. Genesis 3:5.
12. Genesis 3: 5.
13. Genesis 3: 2-3.
14. Genesis 2: 16.
15. Genesis 3:3.
16. Henry M. Morris, *The Genesis Record: A Scientific and Devotional Commentary on the Book of Beginnings*, Baker Book House, Grand Rapids, MI, 1976, p.111.
17. Revelation 22: 18-19.
18. Genesis 2: 16.
19. James 4:7.
20. Genesis 3:6.
21. I Corinthians 13: 12.
22. Exodus 20: 3.
23. Matthew 22: 37.
24. I Peter 5:7.
25. Douglas J. Rumford, *Questions God Asks, Questions Satan Asks*, Tyndale House Publishers, Inc., Wheaton, IL, p. 114.
26. Kerry Walters, *Godlust, Facing the Demonic, Embracing the Divine*, Paulist Press, 2000, p. 26.
27. www.religioustolerance.org/satanis1.htm
28. Deuteronomy 32: 35; Romans 12: 19; Hebrews 10: 30.

Questions for Self-Examination and Group Discussion: Chapter 2

1. If you could talk with Eve today, what would you tell her? What would you say to Adam?

2. What would it be like to have a face-to-face relationship with God? How would your reality be different?

3. In comparison to your answer to question 2, what is the difference in the spiritual vision we have in this fallen world? Give some examples of murky spiritual vision.

4. After the devil asked Eve a question, she entered into a dialogue with him that led her in the wrong direction. What lesson do you gain from Eve's mistake? Have you ever dialogued with the devil (either literally or figuratively)? If yes, please explain, and share the final result.

5. Why is any addictive behavior a form of idolatry? Name some idols from your own life.

6. Have you ever done anything that you knew was not God's will? If you answered no, we'll keep praying for you. If yes, specify an instance or two, and tell why you did this.

7. In what specific ways have you played God?

Chapter Three:

Me-Me-Me

Bear Creek, Alabama, was a paradise for boys—at least that's what I thought when I was growing up. The town was full of my relatives, including many cousins who were anxious for me to join their grand adventures.

Nearby was a creek for swimming and fishing. (Guess what its name is? Bear Creek) There were also plenty of dogs; a horse named Bob; a burro; goats; pigs bearing the biblical names of Shadrach, Meshach, and Abednego;[1] and an affable bull named Charles who let us ride him as if he were a horse.

Everyone in Bear Creek was nice to me and seemed genuinely interested in my life's progress, such as heroic plays I'd made in Little League baseball, new words I learned to spell, and the challenges of long division.

Each year, our family drove from our home in the area of Detroit,

Michigan, to this small town in northwest Alabama, my mother's birthplace. Those trips were the highlight of my summers.

Bear Creek was sort of like Mayberry, only smaller.

One notable difference, however, is that Mayberry was the product of Hollywood script writers. Tragedies were minor in Mayberry and always fixed within the half-hour confines of *The Andy Griffith Show*. But in Bear Creek, a little girl burned to death in a house fire around the time I was born. Her grave in the Bear Creek cemetery is close to the marker of my great-grandfather. During the Civil War, he was one of many from that part of Alabama who fought for the Union. The war there was between neighbors; it was personal and bloody. Also buried in the same vicinity is his son, my grandfather. He ruined his life with booze that apparently drained away his sanity.

A strip of land

There was also a fatal shooting in Bear Creek that left two families without their fathers. It occurred when my mother was a school girl in the early 1930s. Mom was in the same class with a daughter of one of the affected families.

We'll call the two men involved in this crime Mr. Smith and Mr. Jones. They had an ongoing disagreement about the property line that separated their farms. Angry words were exchanged, and things festered.

We're not talking about acres of land that were the subject of this controversy. The focus was on whether the boundary between them should be two or three feet one way or the other.

One of the men moved the marker that separated their land. The other moved it back — and so it went until Mr. Smith moved that wooden stake for the last time.

Armed with a rifle, Mr. Smith hid himself and waited. It was then Mr. Jones' move. When he showed up to make it, he was shot and killed.

Mr. Smith was convicted and went to prison.

Of course, we won't pretend to know what was going on in the mind of Mr. Smith that day as he took aim and squeezed the trigger. Under those circumstances, however, isn't it possible that a narrow strip of land became his false god?

What would motivate the shooting under these circumstances? Before answering that question, let's look at the rational choices involved. One possibility was to maintain the freedom he enjoyed and the ability to provide for his loved ones. Weigh this against death by capital punishment or complete loss of freedom in prison and leaving his wife and children to fend for themselves.

The peeping tom

This reminds me of a choice made by a friend of mine, Steven C. Phillips. (He asked me to use his real name.)

I met Steven when I visited a maximum-security prison to preach at the chapel services in the early 1990s. He had been incarcerated since 1982. In a letter to me, Steven said he was innocent, even though he had been convicted of raping a woman at gun-point. Needless to say, I was skeptical.

He said he'd originally been picked up for exposing himself in public. He bonded out of jail and later read in the newspaper that he was wanted for questioning in regard to the rape. To clear his name for what he thought was a misunderstanding, Steven turned himself in. Little did he know that he would be a prisoner for the next 14 1/2 years.

If you did some quick math, you would have been correct in your calculations if you thought Steven got out of prison in 1996—late autumn to be more exact. He ended up in a halfway house just a few miles from the condo where I lived. I picked him up for church on Sundays.

Steven had been a roofing contractor before his arrest. As a member of the condo board of directors, I prevailed upon the contractor to give Steven a job applying new shingles to our complex.

After three or four days on the job, Steven stuck around after work under the guise of picking up some pieces of tarpaper and shingles that had fallen to the ground. The days were growing shorter as winter approached, and in an early evening shortly after dark, Steven was caught peering into the window of a woman who lived in our complex. I guess the police treated this as more of a nuisance than a crime and didn't press too hard about the identity of the peeping tom. If they had, Steven's parole would have been revoked, and he would have gone back to prison.

Now let's weigh the decision-making process here: Despite years in prison, Steven was in the midst of gaining all sorts of opportunities to make a new life for himself—or he could get caught doing something really irrational and go back to prison. Does this sound anything like the choices we described for Mr. Smith? Is it possible that what Steven thought he might see by peeping into that woman's window — and the accompanying perverse thrill of possibly being caught — had become his false god?

Steven, of course, was fired from the job, and I had to take heat from the roofing contractor for recommending him in the first place.

Steven was embarrassed, and I also told him exactly what I thought about it. After church the following Sunday, I took him to a restaurant where we met with a Christian man whom I knew to be a member of a 12-step group for sex addicts. Steven went to two of the sex-addict meetings, said he didn't like them, and never returned. Five months later, he was caught peeping into the window at an apartment complex. His parole was revoked, and he went back to prison for more than 10 years.

As I write these words in the summer of 2008, Steven has been released from prison and exonerated of all charges against him. DNA tests proved that he was, indeed, innocent of the horrible felonies and also showed that another man who died in prison a decade earlier was the perpetrator. The tragedy is that Steven served more than 25 years in prison on the basis of two misdemeanors that he committed while acting on his own murky perspective.

The wedding party

About a decade ago my former roommate from graduate school asked me to serve as an usher at his wedding. I was honored and looked forward to the trip from Texas to Florida. The bride "Elizabeth" was a native of the New England region, and her parents were flying in from there with her non-identical twin sister, "Emily."

We all enjoyed the wedding rehearsal followed by dinner. Afterward, the prospective bride and groom and some of us from the wedding party had an impromptu get-together in an apartment, where we talked and laughed together for a few hours.

In a telephone conversation to the bride's family at their hotel room the next morning, someone mentioned "the party." Emily, the twin sister, did a slow burn because she was not "invited," although the get-together had been spontaneous and had occurred after she and her parents left the restaurant. She immediately got on a plane and flew home, missing her sister's wedding the following day.

What would prompt such a reaction?

The origin of me-me-me

The three decisions we've discussed above probably all followed instances where something other than the creator of the universe became number one in someone's life—a false god. What do these decisions have to do with Satan?

We know from the previous chapter that Satan was expelled from heaven for trying to take over for God. We also saw that Satan's temptations will reflect—in one way or another—his desire to be God.

Now let's take a more complete look at the biblical passage where God quotes Satan.

> "... I will ascend to heaven;
> I will raise my throne above the stars of God;
> I will sit enthroned on the mount of assembly, on the utmost
> heights of the sacred mountain.
> I will ascend above the tops of the clouds;
> I will make myself like the Most High."[2]

Satan says "I will" five times but never mentions God's will. He was the first to suffer from "I" trouble. Rather than a world-view that is God-centered, Satan viewed himself as belonging at the center of the universe.

Where is God in this picture? We've already seen Satan's scenario for God's place in the universe when he attempted to get Jesus to bow down and worship him.[3]

In short, "playing God" goes hand-in-hand with a perspective of self and the world that is completely distorted. It denies that God is the author of all truth, reality, and spiritual clarity. I've labeled this perspective as me-me-me, but other appropriate terms include self-centered, egocentric, the big I, and ego-run-amok, among others.

Back in Bear Creek, Alabama, if Mr. Smith's false god was, indeed, that narrow strip of land, his misconstrued perception of reality prompted him to trade his freedom and the well-being of his family for a prison cell. A sad irony is that not only did he lose access to the strip of land for which he had murdered, he lost access to his entire farm.

Steven also had a distorted view of reality as he exchanged his freedom for what he might see as a peeping tom. Besides that, his long-suffering mother once again had a double dose of disappointment, and Steven lost his chance to have contact with his children who grew up without their father. I am happy to report that as a free man, he is now addressing the spiritual issues that led him to expose himself in public and be a peeping tom.

Feelings of "less than"

Although different in some ways, Emily's situation shares similarities with those above. Her sister was getting married , and she had no such prospect.

According to her parents, Emily assumed that we purposely

excluded her because we didn't like her or thought she didn't belong. As you already know, this is a huge distortion of the truth. Emily acted upon her murky vision.

Me-me-me always says, "I-I-I am going to make this about me-me-me."

The oversized ego is an easy target for life's slings and arrows. We think of these things in terms of being "thin-skinned" and "overly sensitive." These are a long way from criminal activities. But just as Mr. Smith and Steven were put in prison, these things lead us to a self-imposed solitary confinement where no one can hurt us. Or help us.

If our murky perspective prompts us to perceive that people have hurt us, our logical reaction is to punish them back. So once again, we end up playing God.

From the Bible's great chapter on the subject, recall a few things that are true of love: "It is not rude, it is not self-seeking, it is not easily angered, it keeps no record of wrongs."[4] How do these things stack up to Emily's reaction of returning home prior to her sister's wedding?

How many times have you observed easily offended people react in a manner similar to Emily? I know I've done it. How about you?

Eve's perspective

Who was the first person to use me-me-me in a decision-making process? It was Eve.

Recall from the last chapter that she already knew God's will about the forbidden fruit. Then she heard Satan's version. Here's what happened next: "When the woman saw that the fruit of the tree was good for food and pleasing to the eye, and also desirable for gaining wisdom, she took some and ate it."[5] Focus on the first four words of that verse, "*When the woman saw.*" She then made her decision based on her murky perspective rather than God's truth.

Anytime we let our vision supersede God's wisdom, me-me-me is in charge.

Eve did it, and her descendants have been doing it ever since. One such descendant was the Old Testament King Saul.[6]

Saul played God by ignoring instructions about what he was to do after God gave his army a great victory. The next morning, the prophet Samuel went to talk with Saul about this. He was told, "Saul has gone to Carmel. There he has set up a monument in his own honor."[7]

Godly people build monuments to God, but Saul built one to himself.

When me-me-me is in charge, we will attempt to build monuments to ourselves instead of to God. For Saul, this marked the beginning of a downhill journey that ended with his inglorious self-destruction. Things are no different for us.

The lost son

I identify with Jesus' parable of the lost son (often known as the prodigal son) not only in regard to turning his back on his father but also his trip home.[8] Think about me-me-me and its source as you read what Robert R. Brown wrote to describe why the son left home in the first place:

> There was deep down in the younger son's nature a demonic power which constantly urged him to put self at the center of the universe. Such a condition allowed no place for others because it insisted he must claim every place for himself. He was the sole arbiter of his destiny and his own wisdom was the only judge…[9]

According to Brown, the same "demonic power" resides in each human being. This results in an individual whose estimation of his or her place in the world is greatly exaggerated.

In the words of Brown, "Self does not listen because it is anxious only to be listened to; and self will not salute for it seeks grimly any opportunity to be saluted."[10] Brown also wrote about individuals attempting to "become the gods which our natures whisper we are."[11]

It is easy to see what the prodigal son was whispering to himself. More importantly, though, what do we whisper to our own selves?

A different outlook

What is it like to live in a fallen world? Douglas J. Rumford wrote about the world-view of Adam and Eve after their fall from grace and also described our own perspective through the lens of me-me-me:

> Evil distorts how we see our self and others. We no longer look with pure eyes of appreciation. Now we see each other through the lenses of lust and judgmentalism. We no longer walk in freedom, carefree and accepting of who we are. Haunted by the threat of nakedness, we want to cover up and posture so that others will be impressed. Or at least they won't see our faults.[12]

We've seen how this was evidenced in the lives of Mr. Smith, Steven, Emily, King Saul, and the lost son glancing back at his father in the rear-view mirror. We have no reason to believe that things will be any different for us. What might be different will be the false god we put as number one in our lives and the negative spiritual consequences that follow.

A temper tantrum where a loved one is the victim of our self-centered wrath can result in life-long resentment with cold, emotionless communication or no communication whatsoever.

What are the changes in perspective of a person who turns his/her golf game into an idol? Of putting money as the most important thing in one's life? Of complete dedication to a career at the expense

JESUS' UNIVERSE

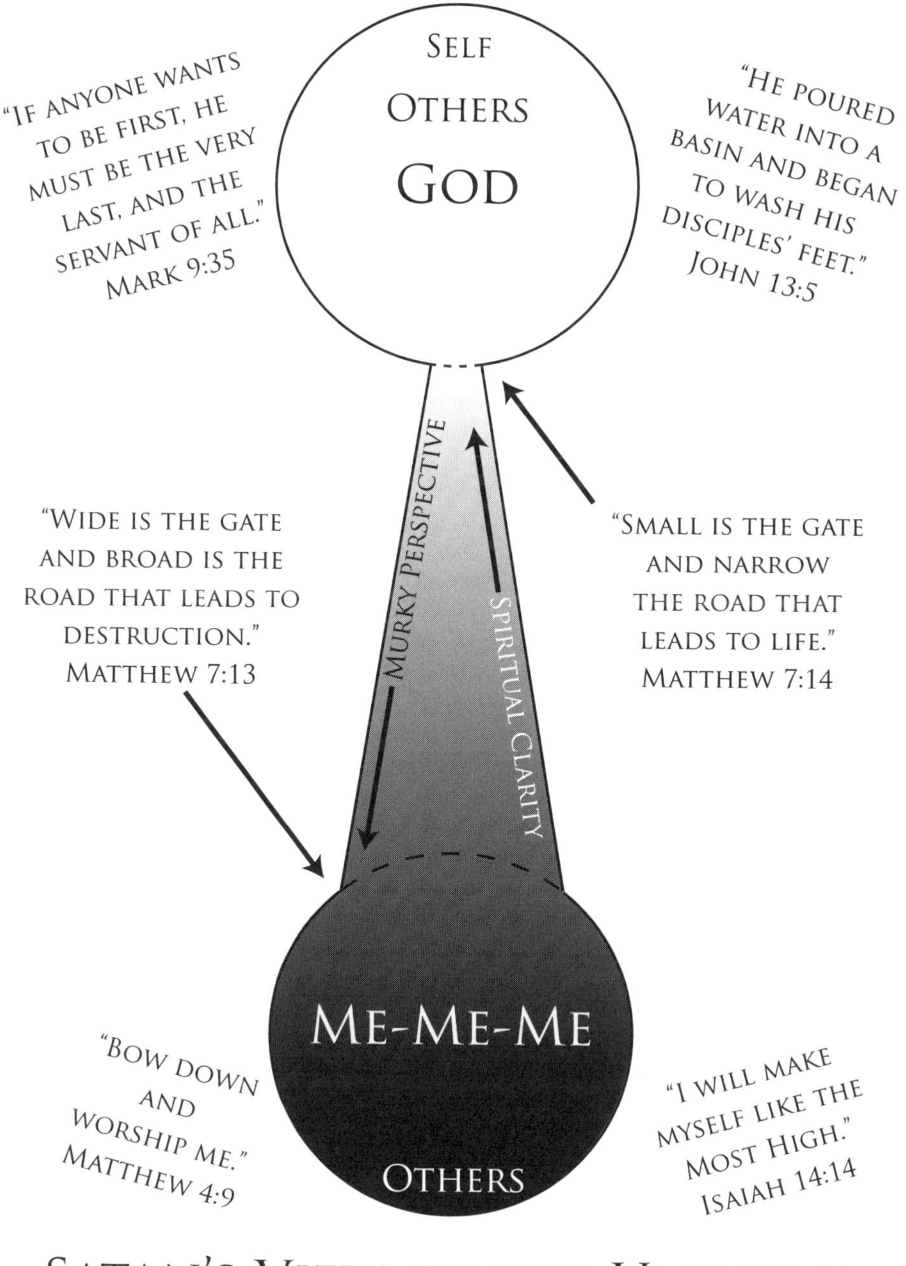

SATAN'S VIEW OF THE UNIVERSE

of one's family?

Just as I drank in high school to overcome fairly normal adolescent anxieties, there are thousands of wrong places to turn to fill the void where God belongs in one's life. When these "false gods" fail to work (which happens 100 percent of the time), the void continues to grow. Rather than seeking the actual solution, we allow Satan to guide us in the wrong directions, and me-me-me continues to enlarge in direct proportion to the void.

Of course, you and I do not live completely in either a God-centered or Satan-centered universe. Only Jesus has been successful in living completely in God's world, and Satan sits proudly in the middle of his illusory universe. These two worlds have a line connecting them, and it is somewhere on this line that Adam and Eve found themselves after sin entered the world due to their actions. You and I reside there now. As such, we have a distorted view of God's world. This is what Paul was talking about when he wrote, "Now we see but a poor reflection as in a mirror. . . . Now I know in part."[13]

The good thing for Christians is that we have a goal to be more God-like continually. Growing close to Him results in increasing peace, serenity, and comfort. The great thing is that Jesus has died for our sins, giving us the assurance of salvation. "Then we shall see face to face . . . then I shall know fully."[14]

If we do not choose to be more like Jesus, we have the freedom to follow Satan's destiny for us while we gain a world-view that grows increasingly distorted as we grow closer to complete self-destruction. This murky perspective goes hand-in-hand with a characteristic of Satan discussed in the chapter that follows.

ENDNOTES: CHAPTER THREE

1. Daniel 1:7.
2. Isaiah 14: 13-14.
3. Matthew 4:9.
4. I Corinthians 13: 5.
5. Genesis 3: 6.
6. I Samuel 15.
7. I Samuel 15: 12.
8. Luke 15: 11-32.
9. Robert R. Brown, *Alive Again*, Morehouse Barlow Co., New York, NY, 1964, p. 23.
10. Ibid., p. 24.
11. Ibid., p. 19.
12. Douglas J. Rumford, *Questions God Asks, Questions Satan Asks,* Tyndale House Publishers, Inc., Wheaton, IL, p. 18.
13. I Corinthians 13: 12.
14. I Corinthians 13: 12.

Questions for Self-Examination and Group Discussion: Chapter 3

1. What are some ways that people can build monuments to themselves instead of to God?

2. Cite an example from recent news events where me-me-me led to someone's criminal behavior.

3. Tell in what ways you identify with "Emily." Give some examples of other ways that manifestations of me-me-me may occur in a person's personal life.

4. Me-me-me is akin to an out-of-whack ego. It has been said that an acronym for ego is "edging God out." For manifestation of temper, "ejecting God out" may be more descriptive. Name some ways that your ego has prompted you to edge (or eject) God out of your life.

5. Thinking about your past, name an instance where me-me-me affected your spiritual clarity and it was only later that you were able to recognize what had occurred.

6. Give an example of a monument that you've built to yourself.

7. Right now, what is the greatest manifestation of me-me-me in your life? How do you think this affects your spiritual clarity?

Chapter Four:

Liar

The 364 days that followed my seventh birthday were marked with growing anticipation and dragged along ever-so slowly. At the age of eight, I would realize my dream and become eligible to join Cub Scout Pack 587 of Detroit, Michigan. Denny, my next-door neighbor who was a year and a half my senior, was already a member and had earned his wolf badge and a gold arrow to go with it.

Unlike the dust-in-my mouth feeling of subsequently "arriving" at anticipated objectives, such as the purchase of a used Corvette at age 23, joining the Cub Scouts was everything I'd hoped for. I was handed a bobcat pin and proudly put it on my new blue uniform trimmed in yellow. I wore that outfit to school each week on the day of our den meetings. These get-togethers were hosted in the homes of den mothers. There were also monthly meetings of the entire pack (several dens equal a pack) in the basement of the Methodist church near Dossin School where most of us attended and which was the starting point for frequent outings when the pack visited somewhere special.

Some of the outings included tours of the Ford Motor Company steel plant in Dearborn, a U.S. Naval base at Grosse Ile, a submarine docked in the Detroit River, and a railroad yard. My memories of those visits are very sketchy. In fact, there is only one incident at one outing of which I still have a vivid memory. It is the trip to the railroad yard. More specifically, it was the opportunity to walk through a red caboose.

How could that be more exciting than watching red-hot molten steel being poured out of huge cauldrons, eating lunch with sailors, or actually entering a submarine?

On the wall of the caboose was a large picture of a smiling woman who was naked from the waist up.

Boobies!!

As we walked single-file through that railroad car, the picture immediately became the sole focus of each Cub Scout.

It was the first time in memory that I'd seen a woman posed in that manner. I'm pretty sure it was about the same for all the boys. This was in the mid-1950s, long before nudity was available routinely on television or motion pictures. And there was no Internet.

I really wanted to stop and stare at the picture for a long time, but my dad was in the line right behind me. Then there was a railroad employee sitting in a chair watching all of the boys gawk at that picture. He looked like he was about to burst out laughing, so, I did my best to play it low key. Looking out of the corner of my eyes, I got the best glimpses I possibly could and kept on walking.

One of my friends was far less subtle. When we exited the caboose, he screamed with exuberance in front of our dads and everyone else, “Did you guys see that? I can’t believe it!” Then, as if he were anxious to return to the most exciting ride at Disney World, he ran to the other side of the caboose for a second tour. I stood there wishing I had the guts to join him.

In the days thereafter, there were some serious, albeit uninformed, conversations on the playground of Dossin School about our observations in the caboose. Of course, it did not occur to any of us that seven or eight years earlier, we’d been nursing on objects about the same as those that we now beheld in amazement.

Women, even though my wife and I enjoy *all* aspects of a good marriage, I’m still not completely sure what “floats your boat” in the sexual area. I’m always astounded at the things you think are “cute.” Between guys, though, there is a usually unspoken recognition that visual stimulation starts early. For pre-adolescents, it is more of a curiosity. With puberty, it becomes sexual. I’m not sure if men reach an age when this goes away. If yes, I’m not that old yet.

I have no reason to believe that things were any different with boys and men who lived hundreds, even thousands of years ago. At some point, though, God-seeking young men are taught that even though there is something in the proverbial caboose they might want to see, it is not in their best interests to act on that desire.

Certainly, a grown man who is a religious leader would know better, wouldn't he? We all know better. Many ministers and priests have fallen prey to lust, and in the aftermath, there is always a price to pay—sometimes it is very public, embarrassing, and harmful to many people.

David's experience in the caboose

David, king of Israel about three thousand years ago, once was described as a man after God's own heart,[1] and he's also the biblical poster boy for lust run amok. From the Bible, it is not clear whether David entered the caboose on purpose or by accident. But if by accident, it is the responsibility of a Godly man to make a hasty exit after realizing the nature of his location.

The fact is that David had stayed at home in Jerusalem when he was supposed to have been miles away leading his army in battle.[2] In doing this, he'd already made a decision to be in the wrong place. Then, "One evening David got up from his bed and walked around on the roof of the palace. From the roof he saw a woman bathing. The woman was very beautiful."[3]

Her name was Bathsheba, and her naked body became David's false god.

As a Cub Scout in the caboose, I was limited in my viewing time of the picture because my father was present. David would have done well to remember the presence of his heavenly father. As David stood fixated on the exposed body of another man's wife, his sole focus instantaneously shifted to his sexual desires (me-me-me). The disasters that followed will be discussed in future chapters. For our purposes here, let's focus on one word: "saw." As in "from the roof he saw."[4] It is no coincidence that this sounds eerily familiar. Recall "When the woman saw"[5] describes Eve looking at the forbidden fruit.

David acted not on what he knew to be God's will in his life, but upon his own vision which was growing increasingly murky with lust. In that way, David "played God" and succumbed to a lie from Satan.

Speaking in the vernacular

It is a well established fact that Satan is a liar. According to Jesus, "When he lies, he speaks his native language, for he is a liar and the father of lies."[6]

Unless the words come from God Himself, the greatest possible lie that could ever be told is this one: "I am God." We already know that Satan tried to "play God" and that this characteristic is at the root of every temptation we will ever face.

Our first view of Satan in the Bible has him deceiving Adam and Eve. Satan asked Eve, "Did God really say, 'You must not eat from any tree in the garden'?"[7]

In fact, as we observed in Chapter 2, those were not God's words. He actually said Adam and Eve were free to eat from any tree in the garden but one.[8] Satan twisted God's words to put a different focus on the issue. Satan's insinuation took Adam and Eve from "You are free"[9] to "God has not given you freedom."

In doing this, the devil attempted to portray God as the universe's original wet blanket. It smacks of "God is trying to keep something from you," and "God is trying to take all of the fun out of your life."

As I turned my back on God and started drinking heavily at age 17, I bought into this lie. I remember thinking that the purpose of religion was to prevent me from really going out and enjoying myself.

When I was having those thoughts (late 1960s), the words "free" and "love" were bandied about both individually and together. Free meant that you were free to do whatever you wanted, including taking supposed "mind-expanding" drugs. Love meant unbridled promiscuity.

Sexually transmitted diseases flourished, and so did drug addiction.

Looking back on it, the vocal spokespeople of the 1960s counter-culture were liars. They were like those about whom Peter wrote who promise freedom "while they themselves are slaves of depravity."[10]

You don't have to be an old hippie to buy into the lie that God wants to take away your freedom and prevent you from having the good times you really deserve. Such perceptions are rampant, even among Christians.

Satan's "Did God really say"[11] question is also an attempt to cast doubt on whether God is truly *the* source of truth. If He is not, where can someone turn? The only alternative is the self-deluded pretender to God's throne, Satan himself.

To Satan's question, Eve replied that according to God, if they eat fruit from the tree in the middle of the garden, they will die. Satan responded with the lie, "You will not surely die."[12]

The rest, as they say, is history.

More than 50 years after gazing at the picture of the half-naked woman on the wall of the caboose, I still have vivid memories of that image. In some ways, the eye-opening experience of this Cub Scout was very much like Eve and David. We all liked what we saw.

A pretty package

This is where the lie comes in: Satan *always* makes sin look good. Remember, Satan masquerades as an angel of light.[13]

Satan offered to give Jesus "all the kingdoms of the world and their splendor"[14] if Jesus would worship him. What Satan offered dwarfed the fame that would go with winning every Hollywood Oscar awarded for a century while making all the money given away by state and mega-lotteries. Of course, Jesus didn't bite.

The rest of us, however, do bite on a regular basis, and the bait we take is much, much smaller but enticing nonetheless. Satan's "strategy is to give people what they want but to make sure they eventually get what he wants them to have,"[15] according to author Erwin W. Lutzer.

There are plenty of other biblical examples that make the same point.

As David gazed down at the naked Bathsheba, how did she look? "The woman was very beautiful."[16]

What is it like to talk to an adulteress? Just great. Her lips "drip honey" and "her speech is smoother than oil."[17] But what would a man discover who gets involved with her? "In the end she is bitter as gall, sharp as a double-edged sword."[18]

How does wine look and how does it taste? "It sparkles in the cup. . .it goes down smoothly."[19] But what is it like in the long term? "It bites like a snake and poisons like a viper."[20]

As you know, alcohol became my false god. What was the enticement? Popularity and becoming a lady's man. Recall that I thought there were a bunch of Romeos at our high school and one big dud, me! That was a lie. As a matter of fact, there were just a few Romeos, and the great majority of guys were in about the same boat as I was. We weren't duds; we were just normal adolescents.

But I turned to alcohol for a quick fix. It seemed to deliver what I wanted, and I can't deny that I had some good times early in my drinking. Even in high school, beer and booze started creating problems in my life, and these problems took over in college.

A friend who is drug-free after many years of cocaine addiction said that he kept using the drug hoping to get the same effect as the first time he snorted it. Of course, he never experienced the same "high," but the quest for it ruined his life.

C. S. Lewis makes this point in *The Screwtape Letters*:

> An ever increasing craving for an ever diminishing pleasure is the formula. It is more certain; and it's better style. To get the man's soul and give him nothing in return—that is what really gladdens Our Father's heart.[21]

(Recall that Lewis is writing as a demon, so "Our Father" refers to the devil.)

Through the grace of God, I've haven't taken a drink containing alcohol since November 6, 1973. My advice to young people about alcohol and drugs is that if they try them, there's a pretty good chance they'll like them, maybe even love them. But I also tell them that those things will put them on a path to destruction.

What do you tell yourself about the effects of sin? Every temptation you encounter initially will seem to have positive benefits for you. When you are tempted, look past the attractive wrapping to examine all the potential ugly contents of the package. Always think of the possible long-term consequences.

"The idols speak deceit," wrote the prophet Zechariah more than 2,600 years ago.[22] Nothing has changed. You can count on it.

Psychiatrist M. Scott Peck defined mental health as "an ongoing process of dedication to reality at all costs."[23] But what is the devil's role? According to Peck, Satan is a spirit of unreality.[24]

Peck was writing about the murky perspective of anyone who yields to Satan. Eve did it, David did it, and so did I.

What about you? How is the evil one attempting to guide you toward a view of the world that is a lie?

We'll explore this further in the chapter that follows.

ENDNOTES: CHAPTER FOUR

1. I Samuel 13: 14.
2. II Samuel 11: 1
3. II Samuel 11: 2.
4. II Samuel 11: 2.
5. II Samuel 11: 2.
6. John 8: 44.
7. Genesis 3: 1.
8. Genesis 2: 16-17.
9. Genesis 2: 16.
10. II Peter 2: 19.
11. Genesis 3: 1.
12. Genesis 3: 4.
13. II Corinthians 11: 14.
14. Matthew 4: 8.
15. Erwin W. Lutzer, *The Serpent of Paradise: The Incredible Story of How Satan's Rebellion Serves God's Purposes*, Moody Press, Chicago, IL, 1996, p. 43.
16. II Samuel 11: 2.
17. Proverbs 5: 3.
18. Proverbs 5 :4.
19. Proverbs 23: 31.
20. Proverbs 23: 32.
21. C. S. Lewis, *The Screwtape Letters*, Harper-Collins, San Francisco, 2001, pp. 44-45.
22. Zechariah 10: 2.
23. M. Scott Peck, *People of the Lie: The Hope for Healing Human Evil*, Touchstone, New York, 1983, p. 162.
24. Ibid., p. 207.

Questions for Self-Examination and Group Discussion: Chapter 4

1. By observing the world around you, how do you know that Satan is a liar? Name some lies that are perpetuated in our society.

2. How and why does a "man after God's own heart," such as King David, fall into sin so quickly and deeply?

3. M. Scott Peck wrote that Satan is a spirit of unreality. Thinking of spiritual clarity compared to the murky perspective of evil, elaborate on Peck's statement and give examples.

4. Temptation to sin is presented in a pretty package. Give examples of these pretty packages and what is concealed inside.

5. What has been a "caboose" in your life?

6. Name some temptations to which you have succumbed that came to you in pretty packages. What did it take for you to find out that the contents of the package did not match the wrapping?

7. Do you currently believe any of Satan's lies? How do you know for sure? How could you ever find out?

Chapter Five:

Denial – Lying to Self

The movie *National Lampoon's Animal House* included many scenes with which I identified. In one of these, members of the "Delta house" fraternity were called to the dean's office in regard to their less-than-stellar academic performances. Pointing his finger at John "Bluto" Blutarsky, Dean Vernon Wormer announced he was being expelled from Faber College due to his 0.0 grade point average. "Seven years of college down the drain!" lamented the dismay-stricken Bluto.

I also was kicked out of college because of low grades. During the first semester of my junior year, I earned a .7 grade point average on a 4.0 scale. (Would you call this a D- or F+?) My undergraduate academic record reveals one grade of "A," and this was only because I had prior access to tests from a fraternity file. Since I did finally graduate after five and a half years, however, I guess my academic experience was not down the drain completely.

During my years as a university professor, I've shared these facts countless times with entire classes. When I did, my students always looked at me with wide-eyed amazement. I then went on to tell them that during my master's and Ph.D. work, I earned a 3.97 grade point average (102 semester hours of "A" and three semester hours of "B").

I liked the idea of giving them "before" and "after" snapshots of my life. Change for the better is always possible, I wanted them to know. I also hoped these admissions demonstrated that as a human being, I was approachable to all students, even those not faring well in my classes.

It is now obvious that my undergraduate performance had a great deal to do with my idea that alcohol was the solution to any problem I might encounter. During my first year of college, I was drunk on one or two weekend nights. Two years later, I drank every day and was drunk several times a week. Since I lived away from home, my parents had no idea what was going on in my life.

It got so that I had feelings of anxiety during my morning classes. Once, I had an anxiety attack during class and ran out the door to the health center. I often had thoughts of impending doom when not under the influence of alcohol.

In contrast to other heavy drinkers, why did alcohol affect me in this particular way? I don't know for sure, but my best guess has to do with genetics. Recall that my grandfather ruined his life with booze. The only time I remember meeting him face-to-face was when he was patient in a state mental hospital. I was five years old and didn't understand the nature of the place we visited that day. My grandfather lost contact with reality prior to his death in 1953.

Even with my own mental problems, I still perceived alcohol as a cure-all. I found that a few beers in the morning quieted my nerves and enabled me to sit through classes successfully. It was during the semester of morning drinking that I got the .7 GPA.

"Seven years of college down the drain!" was a laugh-line for actor John Belushi portraying Bluto, but the ramifications of my dismissal from college felt like my own personal tragedy.

Even worse than my academic failure—at least in my eyes at that time--was the realization that I also failed socially. During my freshman year, it seemed that I was on the fast-track to campus popularity. By the beginning of my junior year, I had received many signs that I was held in low regard, a campus bottom-feeder.

I was baffled. During a time of introspection, however, I compared myself with fellow students and could see that I stood for nothing. I could see that even people I considered as campus nerds stood for something. I might have excelled on the university swim team but didn't bother to try out.

You would think that during this self-examination, I would have questioned the fact that I drank every day. Strange as it may seem, it never once crossed my mind that alcohol was a problem.

In case you wonder where this chapter is headed, the paragraph above more or less defines it—but bear with me for more evidence.

After sitting out for a semester and living near campus as a hanger-on, I took an aptitude test and was readmitted for the following semester. When classes started, however, I didn't bother to attend. I couldn't see any prospect for improvement either socially or academically.

A temporary turning point

I then followed the advice of my mother and applied to a Christian college, where I was accepted. I thus embarked on a new life with simultaneous feelings of superiority and inferiority. The superiority resulted from some misguided notions that my worldly experiences would somehow qualify me for campus leadership. The inferiority was the natural compounding effect of attempting to drink away the insecurities I'd harbored in the first place.

Enrolling in classes at my new campus, I was nervous all the time. I wasn't even sure I'd be able to sit through classes without prior fortification with alcohol.

Oh, about the alcohol, I read in the college manual that students could be dismissed if caught drinking. During my third week there, I found out how serious they were about the no-drinking rule. One night, I got caught returning to the dorm after drinking some beer and faced disciplinary action the following morning.

The only reason I wasn't expelled is that I told them I had transferred there to straighten out my life. I was put on social probation (in addition to the academic probation under which I was admitted), had to go for weekly counseling sessions, lost access to my own car, was kicked out of the dorm, and was told I would have to move in with a minister.

They couldn't find a minister to take me, but they did place me with a nice family, and things there worked out just fine

I really did want to graduate from college, so I took the no-drinking rule seriously. I put on the vestiges of religion and went to church and prayer sessions with fellow students. I wish I could say that I started seeking God with all my heart, but I can see now that I was actually seeking good-looking coeds and campus popularity. Remember, those were reasons I drank in the first place.

After a period of time, it seemed that my religion was working. The anxieties disappeared, and my grades improved to the C+ range. I made a lot of good friends and genuinely enjoyed the Christian college experience. Despite the wrong motivations for my religion, I learned a lot of things that I would draw upon later.

You'd think that I would have compared the two college experiences and come to the conclusion that alcohol was not my friend. But I did not. With graduation in sight, I discovered there were ways to drink and not get caught. Then I returned to daily drinking as soon as I graduated. I stopped going to church just as quickly.

If you thought that all of my previous anxieties came back in spades nearly immediately, you are correct. I still did not perceive a cause-and-effect relationship between my drinking and my anxieties.

I continued to view alcohol as a solution to my problems.

Shortly out of college, I got a job as a newspaper reporter. I won national awards as an investigative report and columnist and was promoted to news-editor when I was 25. Despite the outward appearance of success, I was dogged by anxieties and phobias the whole time. It got so that I was afraid to leave my apartment.

I viewed myself as mentally ill and used booze as a means of dealing with it. I hoped that somehow, someday my mental illness would go away, but I had no idea of why it should go away and no real plan for making things better. I've since learned that the height of insanity is repeating the same thing and expecting different results.

At the age of 26, I visited an internal specialist with the hope of discovering a physical cause for my mental problems, such as low blood sugar. Come to find out, there was not a bodily origin of my problems, but the doctor did discover a bodily effect from drinking. I had an enlarged liver, a giant step on the way to cirrhosis. The doctor said to cut back on booze, and I promised that I would.

In such a circumstance, logic would dictate that I go to great lengths to save my health, but I was beyond logic. I dismissed the idea that my physical well-being was at stake and continued drinking heavily.

At work, I was told that I was going to receive a promotion to be the editor of a much larger newspaper owned by the same parent company. This step-up in my journalism career would require me to move a few hundred miles. Weighed down by irrational fears that were 100 percent valid in my distorted mind, I was horrified by the thought of moving. Rather than deal with this problem, I simply quit my job. I worked as a bouncer in a topless bar for minimum wage and all I could drink. Later, I was employed as a part-time gas station attendant. Talk about downward mobility!

A year after leaving the newspaper, I faced the situation described in the first chapter where I called the suicide prevention center. Shortly thereafter, a friend drove me to a mental hospital. Still looking for some relief, I chugged straight Scotch all the way there. The sad irony is that the booze no longer had any effect. My false god had completely turned on me.

My self-destruction was just about complete.

Denial defined

Did it strike you that despite a mountain of evidence to support the idea that drinking was a huge problem, the obvious never occurred to me?

Why?

The reason is connected to the fact that Satan is a liar. If someone wants to believe a lie and persists in doing so, denial takes over. *Denial occurs when people lie to themselves and then believe their own lies.* This self-delusion indicates that individuals are doing Satan's job for him as they continue on the road to self-destruction.

Below are four interconnected and overlapping conclusions about denial that are supported by examples and scripture.

1. As they walk the murky path toward complete spiritual blindness, people in denial lose all objectivity in regard to themselves. This impacts their view of everything in the universe.

Did you have "rotten egg day" at your high school?

I discovered this phenomenon after walking into the hallway after first-period class one day during my sophomore year. Taking a whiff, it seemed probable that I was the only person in the building who hadn't consumed three or four cans of beans for breakfast. I learned subsequently that the odor emanated from a chemistry class conducting an experiment that produced hydrogen sulfide. I planned to take chemistry the following year and dreaded the horror of having to work up-close with this reeking material.

Much to my amazement, though, when we carried out the same experiment during my junior year, I didn't smell anything unusual. Then I walked out into the hallway and saw many of my fellow students holding their noses and glaring at us exiting the chemistry lab as though we had just detonated the world's rankest stink bomb.

Denial works that way, too. The saying "too close to the forest to see the trees" is completely applicable. Though these things may be obvious to everyone else, people in denial wear blinders in regard to their own problems.

Several months after quitting at the newspaper, I worked as a substitute teacher in the school district where I had grown up. One time, I stumbled home drunk around 3 a.m., and the telephone rang three and a half hours later telling me where to report for school that morning. I had a horrible hang-over but showed up and went about my duties the best I could.

I thought I was acting normally, but word got around the entire school that I was drunk. A teacher at that school was a long-time friend of our family who'd also been my junior high school football coach. He wouldn't give me the time of day when I tried to talk to him that afternoon, and I didn't understand why.

Additionally, two women working in the school office were the moms of guys with whom I'd grown up. I later learned from one of their sons about the way I was perceived that day. I was really embarrassed but apparently not enough to question my drinking habits.

In my denial about the effects of my drinking, I believed that I was under the influence of alcohol only during the euphoric stages of drinking—not when I was in the throes of a hangover a few hours later.

Does the mirror lie?

A recent television documentary on anorexia showed a teenaged girl who had starved herself to the brink of death. She looked like she'd spent World War II in a Nazi concentration camp. Pitifully, she begged for a set of scales to weigh herself because she was afraid she may have gained an ounce or two. That young woman was not permitted to have a mirror in her hospital room. My best guess is that if she looked into one, she would have seen herself as morbidly obese.

I thought my own story of denial was unique, but a nearly identical account was written nearly 3,000 years earlier and appears in the Bible. Quoting from this story in the last chapter, we saw that while wine might look and taste good, this beverage has the following negative effects for someone who over-indulges: "It bites like a snake and poisons like a viper. Your eyes will see strange sights and your mind imagine confusing things."[1]

As this happened to me, where did I turn? Certainly not to God. Rather, I turned to my false god, the very same as the drunkard described in the proverb. His life had turned into a bad dream, leading him to ask, "When will I wake up so I can find another drink?"[2] Now picture this: The man had lost his sanity because of drinking and yet continued to see alcohol as a solution to his problem.

Sounds familiar, doesn't it?

There are similar echoes in this end-times prophecy focusing on:

> …every sort of evil that deceives those who are perishing. They perish because they refused to love the truth and so be saved. For this reason God sends them a powerful delusion so that they will believe the lie…[3]

Speaking of an idol-worshipper, Isaiah wrote,

> …he bows down to it and worships. He prays to it and says, "Save me; you are my god." …He feeds on ashes, a deluded heart misleads him; he cannot save himself, or say, "Is not this thing in my right hand a lie?"[4]

Like the idol worshipper, the object in my right hand (a whiskey bottle) was also a lie. Before realizing that fact, this Humpty Dumpty had to take a great fall. I subsequently came to believe that only God could put me back together again.

2. The person in denial is "always right" and justifies everything he/she does.

Does the Bible indicate that Satan acknowledged he was wrong for trying to take over as God? Did he apologize for leading astray Adam and Eve and their descendants? No and no. We must assume that Satan persists in believing his own lie that his position in the universe is above God who created everything. The devil is in denial.

Reflecting this, people in denial also believe they are correct in whatever they do. As long as they continue in denial, they will not apologize. If they did, it would necessitate that they change the direction of their lives.

Suppose you approach a person whose denial has gotten to the point where his/her life is on the verge of ruin. You say, "Is it possible that you are headed down the wrong path in life?" Or how would I have reacted to that probe during my freshman year of college when it seemed as though the promises of booze were coming true in my life?

Here are some possible responses:

"How dare you judge me by your standards."

"You're crazy."

"Mind you own ______ business and stay out of mine."

What justification did I use to continue my behavior? In spite of my earlier religious training, I professed to be either an atheist or agnostic. It's not that I had conducted an in-depth study and proved to myself that God did not exist. Rather, my lifestyle dictated my new belief system because there was no way to reconcile my activities with the word of God. Therefore, I had to choose between God and the unholy spirit(s), and you know which I took.

In the previous chapter, I cited biblical passages about an adulterous woman whose lips "drip honey, and her speech is smoother than oil."[5] She justifies her actions in the following way: "She eats and wipes her mouth and says, 'I've done nothing wrong.'"[6] Simultaneously, she continues in denial about her direction in life, "her paths are crooked, but she knows it not."[7] "Her feet go down to death; her steps lead straight to the grave."[8]

Using the Bible for denial

Several years ago, I became acquainted with a prostitute, "Abigail." For the record our relationship was not connected with her line of employment. We attended the same recovery group, but her presence there was quite sporadic. When she was there, though, she was very open—in fact probably too open—about her line of work.

On one occasion during a meeting, Abigail mentioned the Bible and seeking God's will in her life. Afterward, I attempted to engage her in conversation about the downsides of her profession from a biblical perspective. Her response was an amazing use of God's word for purposes of self-justification. She told me she was preventing men from committing the sin of Onan.

I had to dig through my Bible to see what she was talking about.

As related in Genesis 38: 1-10, Judah had sons by the name of Er and Onan. Er was so wicked that the Lord put him to death.[9] Judah told Onan, "Lie with your brother's wife and fulfill your duty to her as a brother-in-law to produce offspring for your brother."[10] (This may seem strange to us today, but experts explained this Old Testament custom in this way, "If a man died childless, his brother was duty bound to raise heirs to him by his widow."[11]) This idea subsequently was spelled out in the Law of Moses.[12]

"But Onan knew that the offspring would not be his; so whenever he lay with his brother's wife, he spilled his semen on the ground to keep from producing offspring for his brother."[13] Because of this, the Lord put Onan to death.[14]

Abigail thought it was her job to prevent a host of other men from spilling their semen on the ground and meeting the same fate. Apparently, she was referring to masturbation. She twisted God's word for purposes of self-justification. In doing this, she "played God" and missed the whole point of the story.

By employing this birth-control method, Onan used his brother's widow for his own sexual gratification (me-me-me) rather than fulfilling the duty to his deceased brother that was requested by their father. Ironically, what Abigail offered as a part of the world's oldest profession was exactly what Onan was seeking each time he went to bed with his sister-in-law.

Sadly, Abigail's denial kept her from understanding where her actions were leading. She died a few years later, still a relatively young woman. Twisting the story of Onan was a part of the lie to herself that perpetuated her own personal journey away from God.

3. The person in denial suffers from a loss of identity.

As a drunkard in my mid-20s, I was at my parents' house one day and not under the immediate influence of booze or any drug. I stood staring into the bathroom mirror and asked myself, "Why am I me? Why aren't I someone else?" Then I started pondering the possibilities of people I knew and wondered why I wasn't one of them.

Bizarre thoughts, aren't they? I tried to dismiss them from my mind. I didn't understand why I even had contemplated those questions and certainly didn't know the answers. The only thing I did comprehend was that thinking about these things made me feel really creepy. I wondered whether this was another sign that my mental state was growing worse, another downward rung on the ladder toward complete insanity.

Looking back, I agree that those thoughts did, indeed, reflect a downward step toward a break with reality. But it was not because I had creepy feelings; those things were an effect and not the cause. Rather, the questions were completely valid because at some level, it was my way of acknowledging that I had lost my way in life and had no idea who I was.

So, who am I? The very foundation of that question for everyone goes back to the beginning of the Bible.

"God said, 'Let us make man in our image, in our likeness'. . . . So God created man in his own image, in the image of God he created him; male and female he created them."[15]

This means that the basis of your identity and mine is defined by the fact that we are made in God's image. In order to be true to ourselves, we need to be as God-like as possible.

Since Jesus Christ was God in the flesh,[16] we look to Him as our example. When I asked those unsettling questions about my identity, I had turned my back on Jesus.

Paul quoted the prophet Isaiah[17] in writing the following question: "For who has known the mind of the Lord that he may instruct him?"[18] (The answer, of course, is no one.) Paul followed the question with this profound statement: "But we have the mind of Christ."[19]

Similarly, Paul wrote that people seeking Jesus "All reflect the Lord's glory" (and) "are being transformed into his likeness with ever-increasing glory."[20]

As we seek Jesus in our lives, we come increasingly closer to perceiving the world with His absolute clarity.

Conversely, Paul wrote about the opposite perspective of people who continue in denial.

> The man without the Spirit does not accept the things that come from the Spirit of God, for they are foolishness to him, and he cannot understand them, because they are spiritually discerned.[21]

If we stay in denial, the murky perspective of evil becomes increasingly more entrenched as "our truth." In this manner, one's entire life turns into a self-perpetuating lie to feed the bottomless pit of "me-me-me." This is accompanied by a complete loss of our identity of being made in the image of God.

4. The journey toward spiritual blindness is characterized by a loss of earlier standards and morals.

At some point in my early 20s, a time when I was well on my way toward self-destruction, I gave some thoughts to my personal morality. I lined out some things that would be permissible for me. (Believe me, teaching Vacation Bible School did not appear on this list, but pornography, fornication, drunkenness and the use of certain illegal drugs would be permitted.) Not thinking of myself as completely without morals, however, I drew the line. "I will never do this or that," I vowed to myself.

By the time I went to that mental hospital at age 27, I had done both *this* and *that*.

"Since they did not think it worthwhile to retain the knowledge of God," Paul wrote to the Romans, "he gave them over to a depraved mind, to do what ought not to be done."[22]

The same author described Godless people in this way:

> They are darkened in their understanding and separated from the life of God because of the ignorance that is in them due to the hardening of their hearts. Having lost all sensitivity, they have given themselves over to sensuality so as to indulge in every kind of impurity, with a continual lust for more.[23]

Don't let your eyes skip over the ending of that last passage. "Every kind of impurity, with a continual lust for more."[24] There is a snow-balling effect with denial and "every kind of impurity" feeding on each other. Greater denial leads to greater depths of impurity and vice-versa.

Here's how it worked in my life: The more I drank, the greater the emptiness, which in turn led to greater consumption of booze, ad nauseam on the downward slide of self-destruction.

A confessed sex addict wrote,

> …there was an incessant seeking for that elusive something more/something different that would—or so I felt certain — eventually provide me with that indefinable "it" that would at long last satisfy the craving that burned within me. "It" was always just out of sight and over the next hill and sure to be found on the next website or with the next affair.[25]

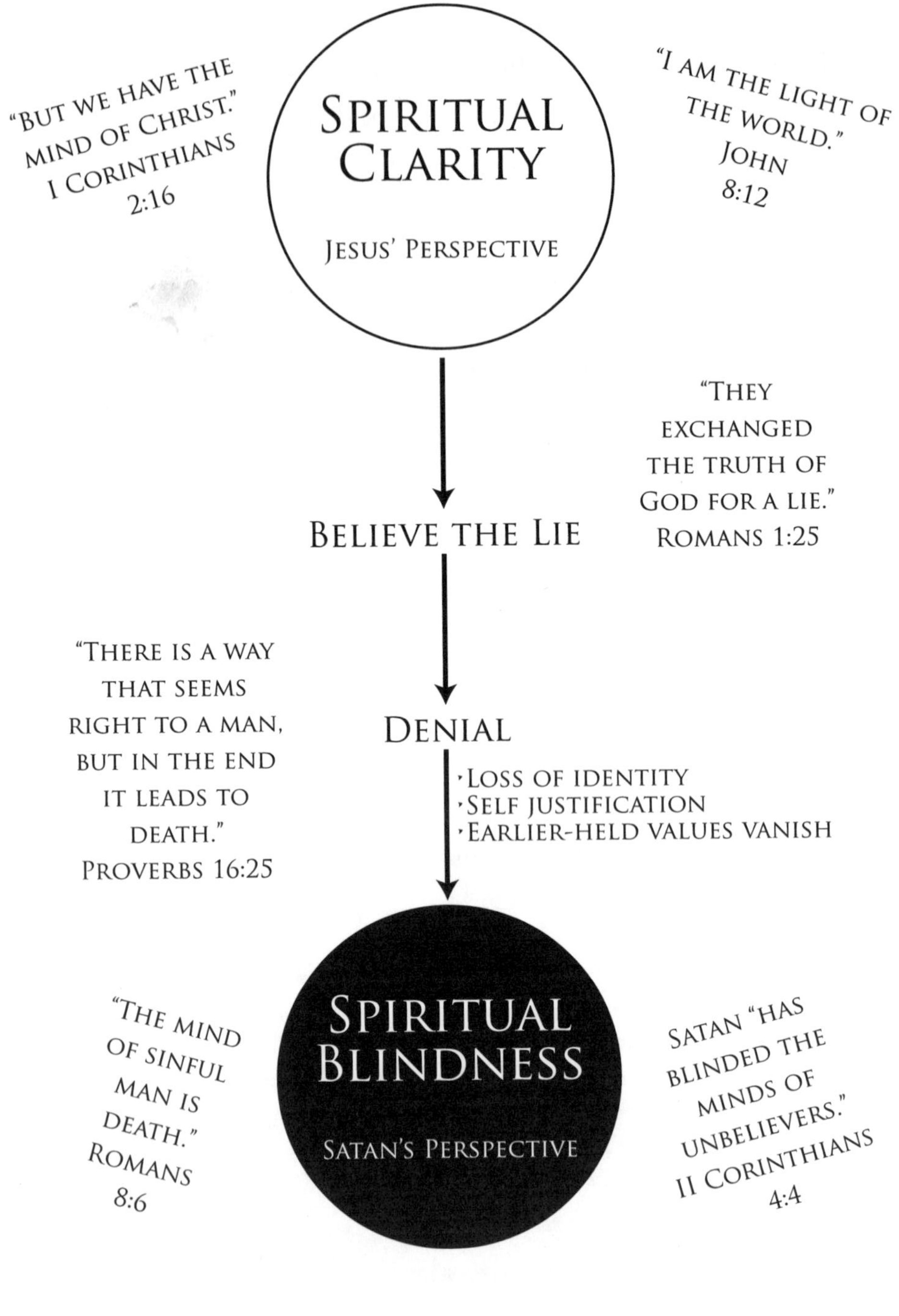
SPIRITUAL CLARITY
JESUS' PERSPECTIVE
"BUT WE HAVE THE MIND OF CHRIST." I CORINTHIANS 2:16
"I AM THE LIGHT OF THE WORLD." JOHN 8:12
BELIEVE THE LIE
"THEY EXCHANGED THE TRUTH OF GOD FOR A LIE." ROMANS 1:25
DENIAL
"THERE IS A WAY THAT SEEMS RIGHT TO A MAN, BUT IN THE END IT LEADS TO DEATH." PROVERBS 16:25
·LOSS OF IDENTITY
·SELF JUSTIFICATION
·EARLIER-HELD VALUES VANISH
SPIRITUAL BLINDNESS
SATAN'S PERSPECTIVE
"THE MIND OF SINFUL MAN IS DEATH." ROMANS 8:6
SATAN "HAS BLINDED THE MINDS OF UNBELIEVERS." II CORINTHIANS 4:4

This man finally realized his search was futile and turned to God.

Attempting to find satisfaction in any false god leads one into a bottomless pit. Yet many deluded people never give up on the search and die trying.

As an individual travels deeper into denial, formerly black and white issues take on shades of gray that grow increasingly darker. The devil would gladly lead you to a place where you commit the blackest of sins while self-destructing in the process.

ENDNOTES: CHAPTER FIVE

1. Proverbs 23: 32-33.
2. Proverbs 23: 35.
3. II Thessalonians 2: 10-11.
4. Isaiah 44: 17, 20.
5. Proverbs 5: 3.
6. Proverbs 30: 20.
7. Proverbs 5: 6.
8. Proverbs 5: 5.
9. Genesis 38: 7.
10. Genesis 38: 8.
11. *NIV Archaeological Study Bible,* The Zondervan Corporation, Grand Rapids, MI, 2005, p. 65.
12. Deuteronomy 25: 5-6.
13. Genesis 38: 9.
14. Genesis 38: 10.
15. Genesis 1: 26-27.
16. John 1:1-3.
17. Isaiah 40: 13.
18. I Corinthians 2: 16.
19. I Corinthians 2: 16.
20. II Corinthians 3: 18.
21. I Corinthians 2: 14.
22. Romans 1: 28.
23. Ephesians 4: 18-19.
24. Ephesians 4: 19.
25. Steve Steele (Editor), *Sex Addiction in the Church: 12 Christian Men Share Their Stories of Recovery,* Quarry Press, Dallas, TX, 2008, p. 73.

Questions for Self-Examination and Group Discussion: Chapter 5

1. Name some specific indications that the author was in denial about the effects of alcohol in his life.

2. Read Genesis 2: 16-17 and Genesis 3: 1-6, and then itemize some ways that Eve was in denial. In what ways is Satan in denial?

3. What is the relationship between denial and the saying, "You can't see the forest because of the trees." How might this show up in someone's life?

4. Think of a character you've observed on television, in movies, or in literature or an actual person in history who did not see him- or herself objectively. What was the difference in this character's view of self compared to the way that others viewed him or her? How did this affect the way others treated this character? What was the net effect of the character's lack of objectivity on the rest of his/her life? (Hint: If you can't think of anyone, from the humorous side of this question, try Barney Fife from *The Andy Griffith Show* or Walter Mitty, the fictional character in James Thurber's short story "The Secret Life of Walter Mitty.")

5. What similarities do you have with Barney Fife, Walter Mitty, or any character who does not look at himself objectively?

6. Itemize some ways that individuals can have identity problems because they lose track of the fact that they are made in the image of God. In what ways during your lifetime have you lost sight of the fact that you are made in God's image?

7. Thinking of your life right now, name some things that stand in the way of you looking at the world with absolute spiritual clarity as if you were looking at the world through the eyes of Jesus Christ.

Chapter Six: Denial in High Places and at Home

Did you get the idea in the last chapter that people in denial lie to themselves? That continuing in denial leads people from murky vision to a complete black-out? That denial paves the road to self-destruction?

If yes, you understand the nature of the problem.

With denial defined in the previous chapter, the purpose here is to provide you with applications to help you recognize denial in your own life. Toward that end, this chapter is broken into two parts.

Part I. A single chapter of the Bible provides a thorough case study on denial in the life of a God-seeking man who suddenly tumbled toward self-destruction. This episode of his life illuminates all the aspects of denial detailed in the previous chapter. In the small-group questions at the end of the chapter, you will be asked to identify those features.

Part II. Just as all have sinned and fallen short of the glory of God,[1] it is certain that everyone but Jesus Christ has lied to him- or herself—and most of us on many occasions. How might denial impact your life, even if you have never strayed too far from God's truth? That question is addressed in Part II.

Part I

In Chapter 4, we referred to King David as the poster boy for lust run amok. As detailed in II Samuel 11, David's lust dragged him into a landslide of denial.

His downward spiral starts with David in the wrong place. He stayed home when he was supposed to have been leading his army in the siege of Rabbah.[2] Then one night while walking on the roof of his palace, David spied on the bathing Bathsheba.

Here's what followed:

a. It is really unwise to act on lust, but after getting a good look at Bathsheba, David sent a messenger to find out her identity.[3]

It is quite probable that David already knew this was Uriah's wife. A hint of this may be found in the way the man answered David's inquiry about the identity of the bathing woman: "Isn't this Bathsheba, the daughter of Eliam and the wife of Uriah the Hittite?"[4] Perhaps that's the way you'd answer a king. In today's parlance, someone might say, "Duhhh, need you even ask? Look, everyone knows her father and husband. Only a moron would even ask that question."

Further, if from the roof of his palace, David could see Bathsheba, you get the idea that she and Uriah lived in close proximity to the palace. Wouldn't David know the identity of his own neighbors, particularly if one of them was one the best soldiers in his army?[5]

If David did know this was Bathsheba, the wife of Uriah, sending the messenger was simply a ruse he was using on himself, a function of his denial.

If David did not know the identity of Bathsheba and her marital status, the messenger's answer took the issue completely out of any possible gray area. It was then time for David to slam on the brakes and turn around, but he didn't.

b. David sent messengers to bring Bathsheba to the palace,[6] demonstrating that his denial was in high gear. The text does not tell how David justified this decision. Perhaps his lie to himself was that he wanted to inquire about the welfare of Uriah. Ultimately, only God knows what went on in his heart, but we can rest assured that it included a lie about his true motives.

c. "She came to him, and he slept with her."[7] Whatever the pretense, it went by the wayside when David got Bathsheba by herself. The adultery moved quickly from fantasy to action.

What about Bathsheba? What was her part in this? I once heard a preacher declare from the pulpit that she had entrapped David. The text gives no inkling that this could be the case, but let's explore this possibility. Suppose that Bathsheba knew it was David's habit to walk on the roof of the palace at night, and she pre-determined to put herself on display for him.

The sin of someone else cannot serve as justification for our own sin. David had to answer to God for his actions, and Bathsheba had to answer for hers. They both failed, but David's failure was greater because he was in the power position as king. He abused the power God had given him.

Further, the preacher's premise contains an assumption that men are completely powerless when exposed to a woman's naked body. In circumstances like David's, our perspectives can get murky, particularly if we are not seeking God's will in our lives. God, nevertheless, has given us a choice, and it's up to us to make the right one.

(If David was suddenly feeling "frisky," couldn't he have visited one of his four wives with the idea of a midnight surprise?)

Then what did they think?

d. After David and Bathsheba had sexual intercourse, she went back home.[8] The Bible doesn't tell us what was going on in their minds. Perhaps David gave himself a mild rebuke and promised not to do it again. But since no one knew about it, no harm, no foul. Right? Oops. God knew about it.

Later, Bathsheba sent word, "I am pregnant."[9]

e. Now David was really in a bind. What could he do? He could confess his sins to God and seek guidance toward some kind of a solution—or he could be devious and try to dupe everyone into believing the baby was really Uriah's.

David's denial took him on the low road as he plotted a cover-up. He sent for Uriah, made some small talk about the progress of the war, and then told him to go home.[10] Wink-wink. "So Uriah left the palace, and a gift from the king was sent after him."[11] Scripture doesn't record the nature of the gift. Do you think it might have been something for his meritorious army service, like a negligee for Uriah to give to his wife?

f. David's plan failed to reunite Uriah and Bathsheba. Why? As an honorable man, Uriah didn't think it was right for him to enjoy the pleasures of home when the Ark of the Covenant was in a tent and his fellow soldiers camped in open fields. So instead, Uriah spent the night in the entrance to the palace with some servants.[12]

Note: "The Hittite" was not Uriah's middle and last name. It designated the country of his origin and the fact that he was not a Jew. Despite this, he was more concerned about the religious significance of the Ark of the Covenant than was David.

g. Confronted by Uriah's honor, maybe it was time for David to start acting like he also had the right stuff. But he didn't. Instead, David went to Devious Plan B: Get Uriah drunk, and he'll forget his notions of honor and stagger home into the arms of his beautiful wife.[13] David undoubtedly knew from scriptures that nothing good came from drunkenness.[14] But even though considerable libation was forced on him by his boss's boss, Uriah still didn't go home.[15]

h. Failing at those plans, David sent Uriah back to the battlefield. As Uriah headed that way with a dry mouth and throbbing head from a hangover, he must have wondered about the actions of his commander in chief over the past few days. Little did Uriah know that the note he was carrying from his king to his general was his own death warrant. In the note, David commanded Joab, his general, to place Uriah in the midst of the fiercest fighting and then have his comrades withdraw from him.[16]

With the failures of Devious Plans A and B, what else was left? Murder.

i. David received word from Joab that some soldiers, including Uriah, were killed as they got too close to the city wall. (Note: Other innocent men besides Uriah also died.) When he received word of this, David passed it off as if the deaths were the result of the vagaries of war.[17]

Now with Uriah out of the way, the way was clear for David to marry Bathsheba.

j. We know that a baby was born of this union,[18] which means that at least nine months had passed since the adulterous union and many months had transpired since Uriah's death. In the meantime, David was still in denial.

k. "But the thing David had done displeased the Lord."[19] So ends the biblical chapter containing the above account.

Of course God knew what David had done, but these events did not occur in a vacuum, and other people must have known about them, as well. The text reveals that David's household servants were at least aware of David's adultery if not involved in the cover-up because he had sent messengers to bring Bathsheba to the palace.[20] Also, it was recorded that on two consecutive nights, Uriah slept in the palace among David's servants.[21] Surely, those servants had some ideas about the reasons for this. And when the alcoholic beverages were flowing the second night, don't you think that some of these same servants were doing the pouring?

Additionally, the general received orders from David to have Uriah killed. Taking these orders were seasoned soldiers who must have questioned the ill-advised military tactics that led to the death of Uriah and other soldiers.

Finally, after Uriah's funeral, Bathsheba married David and moved into the palace. Soon, she was visibly pregnant.

Between all the possible month-counting, speculation, and gossip, isn't it possible that many people in Jerusalem—even hundreds—were aware of what had occurred?

Part II

One night during my mid-teens, I stayed up late by myself to watch a 1940 film on the TV late show titled *My Little Chickadee* starring Mae West and W. C. Fields. It was the first time I'd seen Ms. West. I knew it was true love, similar to my earlier infatuations for Annette on *The Mickey Mouse Club* and Hayley Mills in *The*

Parent Trap. The next day, I told my mother about my new adoration. She then related that her next older brother, Irby, also had idolized the same actress when he was a teen. Hearing that she was old enough for Uncle Irby immediately put the kibosh on my own amorous notions.

As it turned out, Ms. West was born in 1893, making her old enough to be Uncle Irby's mother and my grandmother. She turned 53 the year I was born.

Ms. West was 85 when her last film, *Sextette*, was released in 1978. The storyline revolved around a 28-year-old woman, portrayed by Ms. West, whose five ex-husbands kept appearing during her latest honeymoon. Cast as the other half of the honeymooning couple was Timothy Dalton, born a month before me, who subsequently played the title role in two James Bond movies. Other "husbands" included Ringo Starr, George Hamilton, and Dom DeLuise.

One scene in *Sextette* showed Ms. West walking into a gymnasium and all the musclemen there fawning all over her.

A reviewer for *Time Magazine* said the movie was so bad that it was good.[22] This is about as generous as anyone can be about this film which set out to be a comedy but actually revealed a personal tragedy.

Apparently, Ms. West thought she looked like she was still in her twenties, but her face actually revealed considerable plastic surgery, and it was topped by a big platinum wig. True, she looked younger than her mid-80s—perhaps 10 years younger. Her miscasting was obvious to anyone who saw the film.

Picture her in love scenes with Timothy Dalton, then in his early 30s. On second thought, don't picture it.

Reviews of *Sextette* were overwhelmingly negative. As I wrote this chapter, my wife, Kim, and I watched some clips from the movie. Kim was embarrassed for Ms. West, while I felt myself squirming. But why?

Is it possible that Ms. West in her swansong film, the teenager with anorexia in the previous chapter and I as a 26-year-old drunk substitute teacher are similar peas in the same pod in that we all lacked objectivity in viewing ourselves? Are there ways, perhaps much less obvious, that I still lie to myself and continue to reside in that in that same pod? The answer is yes.

Now here is the painful part: Are you in there with us?

Filling the God-shaped hole in your heart

We all feel there's something missing inside of us. We often forget that this longing is the face-to-face relationship with God that was lost in the Garden of Eden. As a result, we turn to false gods and then lie to ourselves about it. Not one of us has 20-20 spiritual vision. We all have murky spots where we don't see things clearly.

Is it through these murky spots that you view yourself as better than certain others? As worse than others? That you judge others in a vain attempt to conceal your own faults from yourself and them?

Another way to address this same concern is to ask what you are using to conceal the fact that the emperor/empress you see in the mirror is wearing no clothes. As discussed in Chapter 3, this takes us back to Adam and Eve using fig leaves to hide from God after sin entered the world.[23] Douglas J. Rumford was quoted as saying, "Haunted by the threat of nakedness, we want to cover up and posture so that others will be impressed. Or at least they won't see our faults."[24]

What are you hiding behind? A bad temper? Exaggerated stories about your past? A pile of food?

Is your identity always based on the idea that you are made in the image of God? If not, is it based on your golf handicap? Speaking ability? A physical feature of which you are proud?

What is your source of power? Big muscles? Making others feel guilty? Your stock portfolio?

These questions above all reveal forms of playing God. A difference between these examples in comparison to the more blatant ones (e.g., alcoholism, prostitution) is the speed at which we self-destruct. I was on the fast-track in this regard. Others drag it out over a lifetime that spans decades, and they never come out of denial.

A friend of mine liked to say, "You can ride the garbage truck all the way to the dump or get off at any stop along the way before you get there." The problem is that if you stay on the truck long enough, you might actually come to enjoy the smell.

"(There are) those who are pure in their own eyes and yet are not cleansed of their filth."[25] It is not a question of *if* by our own merits that you and I fall into the category of those not cleansed but rather *to what extent.*

ENDNOTES: CHAPTER SIX

1. Romans 3: 23.
2. II Samuel 11: 1.
3. II Samuel 11: 3.
4. II Samuel 11: 3.
5. II Samuel 23: 39 and I Chron.11: 41.
6. II Samuel 11: 4.
7. II Samuel 11: 4.
8. II Samuel 11: 4.
9. II Samuel 11: 5.
10. II Samuel11: 6-8.
11. II Samuel 11: 8.
12. II Samuel 11: 9.
13. II Samuel 11: 12-13.
14. For example, Noah in Genesis 9:21-25 and Lot in Genesis 19: 33-35.
15. II Samuel 11: 13.
16. II Samuel 11: 14-15.
17. II Samuel 11: 25.
18. II Samuel 11: 27.
19. II Samuel 11: 27.
20. II Samuel 11: 4.
21. II Samuel 11: 9, 13.
22. http://www.time.com/time/magazine/article/0,9171,919666,00.html
23. Genesis 3: 7-8.
24. Douglas J. Rumford, *Questions God Asks, Questions Satan Asks*, Tyndale House Publishers, Inc., Wheaton, IL, 1998, p. 18.
25. Proverbs 30: 12.

Questions for Self-Examination and Group Discussion: Chapter 6

1. Any unconfessed sin represents denial. Comment on why you think the foregoing statement is true or false.

2.Denial has been defined as lying to self and believing the lie. How did you see this to be true in the life of King David? How have you seen this in your own life?

3. "As they walk the murky path toward complete spiritual blindness, people in denial lose all objectivity in regards to themselves. This impacts their view of everything in the universe." The foregoing is one aspect of denial discussed in Chapter 5. How was this true in King David's life? How is it true your life?

4. "The person in denial is 'always right' and justifies everything he/she does." By his actions, how did King David demonstrate that he thought his actions were correct? How has denial led you to believe you were correct when you actually were walking away from God? How did you justify your behavior?

5. "The person in denial suffers from a loss of identity." We know that David was made in God's image, the same as we were. As king of Israel, he was also the commander of the army and a spiritual leader. How did David suffer from a loss of identity in each of these roles? How has your denial caused you to lose track of your true identity?

6. "The journey toward spiritual blindness is characterized by a loss of earlier standards and morals." How did this show up in David's life? Name the circumstances from your own past that led you to toss aside earlier held standards and morals.

7. Since denial means that a person does not view him- or herself clearly, how does a person ever recognize that he/she is in denial?

Chapter Seven: Animal

When I was growing up, we often visited Bentley, Michigan, my dad's birthplace located about 150 miles north of the Detroit area. The once-booming Bentley began fading when the train stopped coming through when Dad was a boy. By the time I came along, there was not much left of the town itself but two churches and a couple of broken-down stores. Dad, however, had two brothers and a sister who continued to live in that area.

On a visit there when I was in second grade, Sheba, the cat residing at the farm owned by my Aunt Beatrice and Uncle Clarence, had given birth. We took home a female kitten and named her Tabby. (Okay, it's not the most original name).

A few months later, I looked out the window to see several cats lined up along the sidewalk in front of our house. I pointed this out to my mom and dad, and one of them lamented to the other that

Tabby was so young. I had no idea why this was a problem.

We took Tabby to the animal doctor, known to grown-ups as "the vegetarian," where she was "spaded." Dad had a spade for working in the garden, and it was beyond me as to how the animal doctor would use something like this on a cat.

Nevertheless, he was successful because Tabby came home with a bald spot on her tummy and a few stitches. The cats on the sidewalk never came back.

Suppose rather than keeping her in the house, we had put Tabby outside the night the tomcats were there? There would have been a lot of fighting and screeching, and before it was over, Tabby would have mated with one or more of those cats. This would have occurred despite the fact that Tabby was not previously acquainted with any of her suitors. On this basis, would you conclude that Tabby was a cat of loose virtue? Or would it be more accurate say that Tabby was raped? We'll come back to these questions.

Besides our family trips to Bentley, as mentioned earlier, we also drove south one time each year to the little town of Bear Creek, Alabama, to see my mother's people. On a visit when I was about 11 years old, Uncle Irby's red tractor was parked fairly close to the house. One afternoon, I climbed up to get a perspective from the driver's seat while I ate a sandwich. Boojum and Sport relaxed nearby. These were two of Uncle Irby's dogs, both of them big, mixed breeds and good natured. Sport was "Mr. Personality" and everyone's favorite. In fact, you can find him in the acknowledgments section of a previous book I wrote.

When I was just about finished with the sandwich, I threw a piece of the bread crust to Sport. Boojum suddenly attacked Sport in an attempt to get the bread crust. Locked in combat, the dogs growled viciously and occasionally yipped in pain. It looked like they were trying to kill each other. I was really afraid and didn't know what to do. I knew better than to try to get in the middle of it, which left me feeling not only helpless but guilty for initiating the dog brawl, even though it was unintentional.

Hearing the fracas, Uncle Irby ran out of the house carrying a broom. He somehow stopped the fight, but in the process the broom handle got broken.

It was ironic, I thought, that the dogs forgot all about the bread crust, and neither of them ever ate it. (Of course, being 11 years old, I didn't use the word "ironic.")

Is this for real?

Just before sunset on the same day, I watched as Boojum approached Sport and said, "I'm so sorry that I encroached on your territory. That bread crust certainly didn't warrant my sudden attack on you. I was completely without justification."

"Thank you, Boojum," Sport replied. "It takes a big dog to apologize, and I accept. We've been friends for a long time. I'm sorry, as well. I needed to have followed the biblical principal of turning the other cheek. And I would have, if only I had one—a cheek, that is." Then both dogs chuckled.

Sport then extended his right-front foot to Boojum. As they shook paws, I thought I saw a tear fall from the eye of Boojum, despite some bulldog in his ancestry.

Let me assure you that the above story is true up to a point. And you don't need me to tell you where the fiction started.

Just as the vocal exchange between the dogs is absurd and cartoon-like, using terms such as "loose virtue," and "rape" to describe cat behavior does not ring true, either. These words are associated with bad moral choices that are destructive to self and others. We know that animals don't make choices on the basis of reason but on their instincts.

By attempting to inflict pain, even death, on the other, we know that Sport and Boojum also were acting strictly on instinct. For the same reason, we never would have condemned Tabby for promiscuity if she had mated with several of her suitors, nor would we have pursued rape charges that could have sent the tomcats to the city pound for life.

Ascribing human characteristics to animals made Walt Disney famous in the cartoon world. But if we turn this around and talk about people in terms of animal behavior, it is not cartoon like, and it cannot be played for laughs. Here's an example:

It was in the early evening, just barely dark, when Clay, my friend and co-worker, exited a store in a suburb north of Detroit. Some young men approached and told him about a flat tire on their car.

Although they had a jack handle, they did not have a jack that would enable them to change the tire. Could they borrow his? Clay was glad to oblige.

He opened the trunk of his car and reached in toward the jack. Just then, he was staggered by a vicious blow to the head. Dazed but for some reason still standing, Clay turned around to see that the man holding the jack handle had bashed him in the head with it. The assailant and his companions apparently were surprised that Clay didn't fall to the pavement. Panicked, they ran away. Clay was badly hurt but at least not permanently. He showed up at work a few days later with a pair of black eyes and a huge gash on his head.

Who would risk seriously injuring, permanently maiming, or even killing another person in exchange for the few dollars that might be in the victim's wallet? It would have to be someone so completely absorbed in his own needs (me-me-me) as to be without regard for the consequences in the life of another human being.

Variations of Clay's story appear in the media every day, not only in news stories but also in television programs and movies aimed at entertaining. There's a good chance that you or someone with whom you are closely acquainted has been victimized similarly.

The perpetrators of such crimes—we often call them animals.

Wolf's perspective

Jack London gives us an example of an animal-like individual in his novel, *The Sea Wolf*. This character, appropriately named Wolf

Larsen, is quoted below in a conversation with Maud Brewster, another character from the novel.

> "For look you," he was saying, "As I see it, a man does things because of desire. He has many desires. He may desire to escape pain or to enjoy pleasure. But whatever he does, he does it because he desires to do it."
>
> "But suppose he desires to do two opposite things, neither of which will permit him to do the other?" Maud interrupted.
>
> "... It is the desire that decides. Here is a man who wants to, say get drunk. Also, he doesn't want to get drunk. What does he do? How does he do it? He is a puppet. He is the creature of his desires, and of the two desires he obeys the stronger, that is all."[1]

"Desires" in the above context are the equivalent of instincts in animals. The tomcats in front of our house were acting on instincts. So were the dogs fighting over a scrap of bread crust.

In trying to make a choice between two opposing desires, London has Wolf Larsen saying that people are like puppets. In what way? A puppet has no freedom of action; the string-puller is in charge. Following this logic, a person has no choice in the way he or she behaves; his or her instincts simply "pull the strings." Thus, according to Wolf, humans act on the same basis as animals.

It is true that people may act like animals, but what separates us from animals is that we are made in the image of God. Recall that

God's first three recorded words to humanity were, "You are free."[2] In this fallen world, we continue to have the freedom of choice. We may act as if we are made in God's image, or we may follow Satan and behave like animals.

In the following passage, the New Testament book of James uses the word "desire" similar to the way that Wolf Larsen used it except for adding the adjective "evil":

> Each one is tempted when, by his own evil desire, he is dragged away and enticed. Then, after desire has conceived, it gives birth to sin; and sin, when it is full grown, gives birth to death.[3]

Joe Beam wrote the following about that passage:

> When a person's desire is aroused to a level overruling his logic and noble intent, his want is turned into lust. If a person can be lured into an increased desire, his desires gain the power necessary to drag him away.[4]

In the context of this book, we would say that the desires of a person continuing in denial lead to a spiritual vision that grows increasingly murky toward spiritual blindness. In the previous chapter, we could see that David's evil desire led him to act like a tomcat.

There is no doubt that Satan wants us to deny we are made in

God's image and to behave like animals. To make this point perfectly clear, one of the basic tenets of the Church of Satan is this:

> Satan represents man as just another animal, sometimes better, more often worse than those that walk on all-fours, who, because of his "divine spiritual and intellectual development," has become the most vicious animal of all.[5]

As the fruit reflects the tree, people reduced to animalistic behavior are emulating the devil. The Bible contains numerous references to Satan as an animal and also many portrayals as people acting like animals, all of them unflattering.

Satan is described as a serpent the first time we see him in the Bible[6] and also in an end-times prophecy.[7] It is no compliment to refer to someone as a snake in the grass. Snakes slither along slowly and usually very quietly. They sneak up on their victims. When a snake suddenly snatches its prey, it swallows it whole, slowly and methodically, often while the victim is still alive and struggling for freedom.

Campers have reported waking up to find snakes in their sleeping bags. This gives new meaning to "sleeping with the enemy."

Satan is also called a "roaring lion looking for someone to devour."[8] As a boy, I enjoyed several visits to the Detroit Zoo. Usually, the lions were quite docile, but on one occasion, I was there at feeding time. The powerful cats suddenly got very aggressive. Growling and roaring, they clawed at large chunks of raw meat that were extended to them. This undoubtedly reflected their instincts to quickly overpower their prey in the wild.

While wild dogs will pick out a weak or wounded animal, it is a misnomer that this is true of lions.

> Lions are opportunist hunters, and, after a careful stalk, will take *the closest animal* regardless of its age, sex or condition; they do not test their potential prey for weaknesses, like other predators such as wild dogs do.[9] (emphasis mine)

In other words, any God-fearing individual may be singled out, not just stragglers on the fringes of Christianity.

In end-times prophecies, Satan also is also called a dragon[10] and a beast,[11] both horrifying images of powerful animals.

Twice Jesus refers to the devil or his followers as wolves, each time in relationship to sheep which easily could fall prey to these carnivorous animals. In one of these passages, the Lord likened Satan to a wolf which "attacks the flock and scatters it."[12] The other is a reference to a wolf in sheep's clothing. This comes from Jesus' description of false prophets.[13] On the outside, they look like peaceful bearers of God's word, but this disguises the fact that right under the facade is a vicious animal. In short, their appearance is a lie.

The book of Jeremiah uses animal images to describe men who worship false gods and visit prostitutes. "They are well-fed, lusty stallions, each neighing for another man's wife."[14] Is this the derivation of the term "unbridled lust?"

The Bible also compares people to dogs. One such reference is to people taking part in the execution of Jesus. It is contained in an amazing prophecy written by David which includes many details of Christ's crucifixion written a thousand years before the actual event. "Dogs have surrounded me; a band of evil men has encircled me, they have pierced my hands and my feet."[15]

Among the final verses in the Bible, Satan's followers also are referred to as dogs.

> Blessed are those who wash their robes, that they may have the right to the tree of life and may go through the gates into the city. Outside are the dogs, those who practice magic arts, the sexually immoral, the murderers, the idolaters and everyone who loves and practices falsehood.[16]

Peter gave us a chilling description of people who follow "The corrupt desire of the sinful nature and despise authority"[17] as "Brute beasts, creatures of instinct, born only to be caught and destroyed."[18]

Besides criminal and sexual behavior, how might individuals act like animals in everyday life?

What about venomous language? A person in a state of rage? Eating like a pig?

From *Whom* or *What* Are You Descended?

How would it affect a society's behavior if people thought they were descended from animals? There are plenty of examples in contemporary society.

The prevailing "scientific" theory of our origins states that we evolved from animals. This idea may be found in the writings of Charles Darwin during the 19th Century. Here is what Darwin wrote in his 1858 *Autobiography*:

> A man who has no assured and ever present belief in the existence of a personal God or of future existence with retribution and reward, can have for his rule of life, as far as I can see, only to follow those impulses and instincts which are the strongest or which seem to him the best ones. A dog acts in this manner, but he does so blindly. A man, on the other hand, looks forwards and backwards, and compares his various feelings, desires and recollections.[19]

According to Darwin, there is no reason to act on a belief that God exists. Therefore, like dogs or Jack London's character Wolf Larsen, people act on behalf of their instincts. Darwin separates people from dogs on the basis of a capacity for "feelings, desires and recollections." These things are subjective in that they vary from person to person. Such ideas have led to moral relativism where there is no big truth but many individual truths and each person is his/her own god.

In a 1989 essay, well-known evolution defender Richard Dawkins, a zoologist at Oxford University, observed that Darwin shocked "the vanity of our species" when he showed that people are "close cousins to. . . monkeys and apes," and concluded that "we too are animals."[20]

Does a wide-spread belief that we are descendants of animals account for all the ills of our society? No, not by itself. But a starting point as to what defines the very core of humanity not only affects the journey but also the destination.

Think of two possible starting points: 1. God spoke the universe into existence, and you are made in the image of God. 2. You are descended from animals, and there is no God. How would each of these determine your day-to-day life choices? A wide-spread belief in the second proposition has led us on a journey away from God to the point where we now have arrived.

Darwin's theory is the creation story for atheism. Satan must rejoice in this accomplishment.

Act or React?

As observed, humans have dual natures. While animals react to their instincts, we may either react on the basis of our desires/instincts, or we may act as though we are made in God's image. We have a choice because God has given us free will.

Let's look at how this might work. Residing in Dallas, Texas, I often am confronted with the perils of big city traffic. This includes some rude and inconsiderate drivers and some people who are not paying full attention.

Suppose I'm not the rude driver and I am paying attention as I journey on a freeway. Driving at 55 mph, I have left ample room between myself and the car in front of me. The driver beside me suddenly darts into the space in front of me, sees that traffic ahead is starting to slow, and hits his brakes. I slam on mine to avoid rear-ending him.

What happens next? Let's look at two possibilities and their end results.

1. I say to myself quietly, "God bless that man" and instantly offer a short prayer on his behalf.

What are the final results? It does not matter whether he was actually a rude driver or whether it was only my perception that he was in the wrong. By asking for God's blessings on that man, he is in God's hands. I do not have to think about him any more. I retain the freedom of choice that God has given me and continue in the same direction I was headed originally.

2. The little space that had been in front of me becomes number one in my life. (A false god.) The thought darts into my head. "How dare this driver do this to me-me-me!" I instantly determine that this man needs to be punished for what he has done. (Playing God.) I proceed to punish him by tail-gating accompanied by ongoing blasts of my horn and obscenities from my mouth. I even

throw in a few obscene gestures to get my point across.

What are the results of this second option? There are a whole lot of possibilities, none of them good. Even if the bad driver's actions were not focused on doing something to inconvenience me (and they probably weren't), I make them about me-me-me and act according. He and I could have words, a fight, or worse. My reactions could cause an accident where people are injured or killed, even innocent third parties.

While I am reacting, adrenaline pumps into my body, creating the well-known "fight or flight" syndrome. Physiological changes occur (increased perspiration, respiration, pulse rate, and blood pressure) and even if there are no other negative ramifications of my reactions, I still suffer.

I recall the incident several times later and get upset each time. By reacting (like animals do), I have lost my freedom of choice. The other driver's actions have dictated my reactions. By reacting, I am no different than Boojum attacking Sport over a crust of bread.

In the Sermon on the Mount, Jesus addressed the idea of acting when someone is really in a circumstance where he/she feels like reacting.

> If someone strikes you on the right cheek, turn to him the other also. And if someone wants to sue you and take your tunic, let him have your cloak as well. If someone forces you to go one mile, go with him two miles.[21]

Jesus not only spoke it, he lived it. As Peter wrote of his Master,

> When they hurled their insults at him, he did not retaliate; when he suffered, he made no threats. Instead, he entrusted himself to him who judges justly.[22]

The idea of acting instead of reacting is connected to Jesus' statement, "Everyone who sins is a slave to sin."[23] As God's children, we have the freedom to act, but Satan wants to us to be slaves to anything but God. Someone or something starts pulling our strings, and we become the puppets that Wolf Larsen described. As slaves, we can only react to the sin.

I have observed people who seem to have no agenda of their own. Their whole lives are filled with reactions to people, places, and things. They are like the steel ball in the pinball machine which continually contacts bumpers or flippers and each time goes careening in another direction.

Here are a few possible situations where we might have a tendency to react:

- Someone says something that we don't like. We could spend the rest of the day thinking about this, talking about it with others, and calculating a reaction to the alleged offender.
- Our boss does not give us the raise we were expecting. We could have a bad attitude for days, weeks, even years to come. We might determine to give less effort in our workplace in the future.

- We either have been subjected (or perceive we have been subjected) to abuse, crime, discrimination, a dysfunctional home, etc. Thereafter, our identity is wrapped up in being a victim, and it prevents us from doing something positive on our own behalf.

Jesus doesn't want us going through our lives as puppets to sin, anger, and resentments. That's why he told us, "Love your enemies and pray for those who persecute you."[24]

Douglas J. Rumford wrote,

> Jesus knew what we all had to learn. Unless we intentionally stop and spend time with God, we will always be reacting to the world, doing what other people want us to do or being controlled by our own desires. The world, other people's agendas and our own desires can be very dangerous.[25]

Endnotes: Chapter Seven

1. Jack London, *The Sea Wolf*, Signet Classic, New York, NY, 1964, p. 193-194.
2. Genesis 2: 16.
3. James 1: 14-15.
4. Joe Beam, *Seeing the Unseen Revised*, Howard Books, New York, NY, 2000, p. 155.
5. www.theisticsatanism.com/politics/LaVey/9_statements.html
6. Genesis 3: 1.
7. Revelation 20: 2.
8. I Peter 5: 8.
9. http://home.intekom.com/ecotravel/Guides/Wildlife/Vertebrates/Mammals/Big5/Lion/african-lion-hunting-habits.htm
10. Revelation 12: 7-12; 13: 2-8.
11. Revelation 13: 11-18.
12. John 10: 12.
13. Matthew 7: 15.
14. Jeremiah 5: 8.
15. Psalm 22: 16.
16. Revelation 22: 14-15.
17. II Peter 2: 10.
18. II Peter 2: 12
19. http://www.update.uu.se/~fbendz/library/cd_relig.htm
20. Richard Dawkins, "Darwinism and Human Purpose," in *Human Origins* (John R. Durant, Editor), Clarendon Press, Oxford, U.K., 1989, pp. 137-138.
21. Matthew 5-39-41.
22. I Peter 2: 23.
23. John 8: 34.
24. Matthew 5: 44.
25. Douglas J. Rumford, *Questions God Asks, Questions Satan Asks,* Tyndale House Publishers, Inc., Wheaton, IL, 1998, p. 134.

Questions for Self-Examination and Group Discussion: Chapter 7

1. What are some ways—subtly or obviously/metaphorically or actually--that someone attending church each Sunday might act like an animal?

2. As described by Charles Darwin, "survival of the fittest" is a mechanism at work in the evolutionary process of one animal evolving into another and eventually accounting for mankind upon the earth. How might this mechanism show up in the life of a wolf living in the wild? In terms of human behavior? How does "survival of the fittest" conflict with the teachings of Jesus Christ?

3. Based on what he told Maud Brewster in this chapter, what could you tell Wolf Larsen that would be helpful to him?

4. Read Jesus' story of the Good Samaritan from Luke 10: 30-37. Name who acted like an animal and who didn't. Make sure to support each of your answers with specific reasons.

5. What is the difference between reacting and responding? Give some examples of when you have reacted. . . Of when you have responded. What were the outcomes of each?

6. In today's society, what are some practical applications of when we could "turn the other cheek." Think of an instance when you needed to do this but didn't. What prevented you? If similar circumstances were repeated later today, tell how you would do better.

7. Looking to your past, name an instance when you—in one way or another—acted like an animal. What triggered this? How long did it take for you to come out of denial about this? What enabled you to come out of denial?

Chapter Eight:

Backward

See if you can answer this question before you continue: Whose tombstone is inscribed with these words?

> Once an infidel and libertine. . .by the rich mercy of our Lord and Saviour Jesus Christ, preserved, restored, pardoned, and appointed to preach the faith he had long labored to destroy.

Hint: You are probably familiar with a church hymn written by this man.

Another Hint: The title of this hymn has to do with grace.

Last Hint: We're talking about grace that is amazing.

Buried beneath that grave marker is the former slave trader, British-born John Newton, who wrote "Amazing Grace" and many other church hymns. He was 82 when he died in 1807.

Before losing his mother while still a boy, Newton received some religious instruction. In the years that followed, however, he turned his back on God. On May 10, 1748—a month shy of his 23rd birthday—Newton, as captain of a slave-ship, encountered a storm during a return voyage from America. The sea was so violent that he was certain he would be lost along with the ship and its crew. In desperation, Newton cried out, "Lord have mercy upon us!"

Making it safely through the storm, Newton reflected on the words that had come out of his mouth. He came to believe that it was only through God's grace that he had been spared. Newton viewed this date as his "great deliverance" and observed its anniversary for the rest of his life. Years later, he reflected on that day when he wrote the third verse of the hymn "Amazing Grace:"

> Thro' many dangers, toils and snares,
> I have already come;
> 'tis grace has bro't me safe thus far,
> and grace will lead me home.

The first verse of the same hymn summarizes his spiritual journey and continues to bear testimony to millions of people:

> Amazing grace! (how sweet the sound)
> That sav'd a wretch like me!
> I once was lost, but now am found,
> Was blind, but now I see.[1]

Along with many others, I identify strongly with the message of grace. Like Newton, I reached a point where in desperation I called out, "Help me, God!" This occurred when I was about 25 at a moment when it seemed that my anxieties soon would overtake me completely. Later, I remember thinking how strange it was that I would call to God for help while at the same time claiming to be an atheist.

I pondered that inconsistency. As I later grew spiritually, I came to realize why a professed atheist would call out to God. Being made in His image, there was deep down inside of me a basic understanding of God's presence. At the most basic level, I still knew that God was my only hope.

Unlike Newton, my plea to God was not my day of deliverance. I continued drinking in misery for two more tumultuous years.

A new vision

In May 1974, when I had six months of sobriety, I found out first-hand about Newton's words, "Was blind, but now I see." This occurred as I traveled in my car along Outer Drive, a thoroughfare that meanders around metropolitan Detroit. I was on a section with three lanes going each direction divided by a broad grassy area and other vegetation.

In Michigan's climate, April showers really do bring on May flowers. I looked to my left and saw a large patch of tulips in full bloom. I was awestruck by their colors and beauty. It was as if at age 28, I was beholding a flower for the very first time in my life. Upon seeing those flowers, I knew immediately that I was looking at the world differently.

I came to realize that I had been blinded to God's truth and beauty like the wine-bibbing party-goers described in Isaiah "They have no regard for the deeds of the Lord, no respect for the work of his hands."[2]

When writing "Was blind, but now I see," Newton may have been thinking about the following biblical passage:

> The god of this age has blinded the minds of unbelievers, so that they cannot see the light of the Gospel of the glory of Christ, who is the image of God.[3]

Of course, "The god of this age" is Satan.

Spiritual blindness occurs when the murky perspective of evil takes over completely. This may happen with continuing denial over a long period of time—or it may occur nearly instantaneously as it did with David leering at the bathing Bathsheba.

People who are spiritually blind are led by the evil one in a direction that is directly away from Jesus. So, for example, if the Lord would be found at due north, Satan would lead people due south. If Jesus were up, Satan would lead them downward. People continuing in denial and blinded to God's truth have no idea where they are headed.

Compass anyone?

After making some observations of the world around you, have you ever had the feeling that things were backward? Maybe you were right. In Satan's world, things are backward. Starting in the Bible, there is plenty to back up this notion.

God said in the First Commandment, "You shall have no other gods before me."[4] Satan claims to be God.

God is the author of all truth. Satan wants us to think his lies are the truth.

"'As surely as I live,' says the Lord, 'every knee will bow before me; every tongue will confess to God.'"[5] Satan wanted Jesus to bow down and worship him[6] and yearns for the same thing from us.

"You are free" are God's first three words to humanity.[7] Satan would have us be slaves.

Throughout the Bible, there is a recurring theme of light and darkness as being the polar opposites of good and bad. God "Lives in unapproachable light."[8] "God is light; in him there is no darkness at all."[9] Jesus said, "I am the light of the world. Whoever follows me will never walk in darkness, but will have the light of life."[10]

Evil is described as darkness,[11] and so is hell.[12] As Jesus was arrested in the Garden of Gethsemane prior to his crucifixion, he stated, "This is your hour—when darkness reigns."[13] When He was crucified later, darkness covered the land.[14]

Backward thinking is evident in other passages.

"Woe to those who call evil good and good evil, who put darkness for light and light for darkness, who put bitter for sweet and sweet for bitter."[15] Why "woe?" Because they are listening to Satan's glib, deceitful words and have everything backward.

Referring to godless, wicked people, Paul wrote: "Although they claimed to be wise, they became fools."[16] "They exchanged the truth of God for a lie."[17] They have things backward.

Despite the fact that he thought he was serving God, Saul of Tarsus walked in spiritual darkness and had things backward because he thought it was his role to persecute and kill Christians. Going about this business, "Suddenly a light from heaven flashed around him."[18] This was the light of Jesus who spoke to him saying, "Saul, Saul, why do you persecute me?"[19] The light was so strong that it blinded Saul. He spent the next three days in prayer and fasting.[20] It was then that he was ready for the spiritual truth brought to him by Ananias.[21] The end to Saul's physical and spiritual blindness came at the same time. Subsequently, Saul had a new identity and became known as Paul.[22]

I had it backward

No matter how low drinking took me, denial kept me thinking that alcohol was the solution and God was the problem when the actual truth was just the opposite. I had things backward and not just in perceptions of alcohol's role in my life.

While drinking, I thought my problems were the fault of my

parents, but I was the one pouring alcohol down my throat—not them.

I resented a former girlfriend and perceived that she had treated me poorly. As I later sought God's truth in my life, I came to see that I had this backward—she was a fine young lady who did nothing to earn the spiteful treatment that she received from me.

Having worked with addicted individuals, I have observed that their problem-solving skills often are backward. They may recognize that something is wrong in their lives, but their "solution" often makes the problem even worse. It is only after they get clean and sober that the fog starts to clear and they start to recognize real solutions.

Over the past two decades, a lot of attention has been focused on what is called The New Age Movement. Erwin W. Lutzer wrote that people subscribing to this philosophy believe that the "fall" of humanity in the Garden of Eden was actually upward.

> New Agers teach that the serpent and the woman are the redeemers because their act bought about man's enlightenment. It was, after all, the fruit of the tree that gave them this special knowledge which had been hidden from them.[23]

Any doubt now about the source of this movement?

On the following page are some rules of behavior taken from the Church of Satan.[24] Beside each of these rules is a Bible quotation on the same subject.

Read these and decide which is backward:

Church of Satan

Prayer is useless; it distracts people from useful activity.

Members enjoy indulgence instead of abstinence. They practice with joy all the seven deadly Christian sins (greed, pride, envy, anger, gluttony, lust and sloth).

If a man smites you on one cheek, smash him on the other.

Do unto others as they do unto you.

Engage in sexual activity freely, in accordance with your needs (which may be best realized either through monogamy, or by having sex with many others; through heterosexuality, homosexuality or bisexuality; using sexual fetishes as you wish; by yourself or with one or more consenting adults. The ideal is a monogamous relationship based on compatibility and commitment.

Bible Quotation

Pray for each other so that you may be healed.
The prayer of a righteous man is powerful and effective.[25]

But the fruit of the Spirit is love, joy, peace, patience, kindness, goodness, faithfulness, gentleness and self-control. Against such things there is no law. Those who belong to Christ Jesus have crucified the sinful nature with its passions and desires. Since we live by the Spirit, let us keep in step with the Spirit. Let us not become conceited, provoking and envying each other.[26]

Do not resist an evil person. If someone strikes you on the right cheek, turn to him the other also.[27]

Do to others what you would have them do to you, for this sums up the Law and the Prophets.[28]

Do not be deceived: Neither the sexually immoral nor idolaters nor adulterers nor male prostitutes nor homosexual offenders. . .will inherit the kingdom of God. [29]

God is love,[30] and the Bible contains what is known as the great passage on love.[31] Below is a backward paraphrase of that passage that provides some clear descriptions of Satan and even helps to define the evil one.

> Hate is not patient, hate is not kind. It does envy, does boast, it is proud. It is rude and self-seeking, it is easily angered, it keeps a record of all wrongs. Hate delights in evil but laments at the truth. It never protects, never trusts, never hopes, and never perseveres. Hate always fails. . . .

If you want to find out Satan's will for your life, turn around any biblical principle. Start with these:

"We live by faith, not by sight."[32]

"Do not judge, or you too will be judged."[33]

"Therefore I tell you, do not worry about your life, what you will eat or drink; or about your body, what you will wear. Is not life more important than food, and the body more important than clothes?"[34]

"Love your enemies, do good to those who hate you, bless those who curse you, pray for those who mistreat you."[35]

Is it clear that Satan has things backward? That he wants you to be blinded spiritually and wants to lead you away from your Savior?

ENDNOTES: CHAPTER EIGHT

1. Newton information taken from www.texasfasola.org/biographies/johnnewton and www.joyfulheart.com/misc/newton.htm
2. Isaiah 5: 12.
3. II Corinthians 4: 4.
4. Exodus 20: 3.
5. Romans 14: 11; Isaiah 45: 23.
6. Matthew 4: 9.
7. Genesis 2: 16.
8. I Timothy 6: 16.
9. I John 1:5.
10. John 8: 12
11. Romans 13: 12; Eph. 5: 8, 11.
12. Matthew 22: 13; Matthew 25: 30.
13. Luke 22: 53.
14. Matthew 27: 45; Mark 15: 33; Luke 23: 44.
15. Isaiah 5:20.
16. Romans 1: 22.
17. Romans 1: 25.
18. Acts 9: 3.
19. Acts 9: 4.
20. Acts 9:9.
21. Acts 9: 17-18.
22. Acts 13:9.
23. Erwin W. Lutzer, *The Serpent of Paradise: The Incredible Story of How Satan's Rebellion Serves God's Purposes,* Moody Press, Chicago, IL, 1996, pp. 45-46.
24. http://www.religioustolerance.org /satanis1.htm
25. James 5: 16.
26. Galatians 5: 22-25.
27. Matthew 5: 39.
28. Matthew 7: 12.
29. I Corinthians 6: 9-10.
30. I John 4: 8.
31. I Corinthians 13: 4-7.
32. II Corinthians 5:7.
33. Matthew 7:1.
34. Matthew 6: 25.
35. Luke 6: 27-28.
36. II Corinthians 5:7.

Questions for Self-Examination and Group Discussion: Chapter 8

1. David wrote in Psalm 8: 3 that he came to a closer understanding of God's majesty when he considered the vast sky at night and saw the moon and the stars which God had set in place. The author of this book said that he knew he was in the midst of a spiritual awakening by seeing the color and beauty in flowers. Name some ways that you have perceived the work of God's hands by looking at God's creation.

2. "We live by faith, not by sight."[36] In what way did Eve live by sight? (Hint: See Genesis 3:6) Name some ways that people may be led astray by living by their own sight.

3. When you look in the world around you, what are some things that you know are backward?

4. Name some ways that Christians can get things backward.

5. The author wrote that he once called out to God during a time of anxiety, even though at the time he professed to be an atheist. He subsequently concluded that he did this because deep down inside of every person is an idea about the presence of God. Have you observed this phenomenon to be true in your own life or in the lives of people around you? If yes, give some examples.

6. There are many ways for spiritual blindness to overtake a person immediately. As described in this chapter, lust took over immediately when David saw Bathsheba bathing. Anger also may cause immediate spiritual blindness. Name some more examples of how this may occur, and describe how you have fallen prey to immediate spiritual blindness. How did you feel about yourself afterward?

7. Describe a period in your own life when you had things backward as a result of ongoing denial. What did it take for you to recognize this fact and get back on course?

Chapter Nine:

Self Destruction

Jerry Garcia, lead singer of the Grateful Dead, was a Pied Piper of the hippie era in the 1960s. Three decades later, he and the group still had legions of devotees calling themselves "Deadheads." Many of them followed the band to concert venues throughout the country and advocated drug use as a means of enhancing the concert experience.

"Hell in a Bucket" was a song introduced during Grateful Dead concert tours in 1983, and a recorded version was released four years later. It contains the lyrics that say, in effect, the journey to hell is an enjoyable one.

The first time I heard "Hell in a Bucket," its words did not ring true from my experiences. It is also hard to imagine that Jerry Garcia, a long-time heroin addict and diabetic, really believed them either. He was 53 when he died of heart failure at a drug treatment facility in California.[1]

The message of "Hell in a Bucket" is not unique. Its basic idea is repeated in many ways, some of them subtle, some not. The completely blatant "Highway to Hell" by AC/DC refers to hell as the Promised Land.

It may or may not be true that the road to hell is paved with good intentions, but there is no mistaking that things are backward when this trip is glorified and the final destination is called "the Promised Land."

As a part of the lie, Satan wants to make the self-destructive journey as attractive as possible.

The trip to the original Promised Land was led by Moses as he guided the children of Israel out of slavery in Egypt. This was no Sunday afternoon excursion. It included ongoing rebellion against God and plenty of complaining that extended the trip to 40 years.

When the children of Israel were finally on the verge of entering the Promised Land, Moses talked to them about the opposing choices they would face in the future.

> "I have set before you life and death, blessings and curses. Now choose life, so that you and your children may live and that you may love the Lord your God, listen to his voice, and hold fast to him. For the Lord is your life."[2]

How does an individual choose the curses on the path to self-destruction? Moses was clear that they result from "playing God."

> "But if your heart turns away and you are not obedient, and if you are drawn away to bow down to other gods and worship them, I declare to you this day that you will certainly be destroyed."[3]

The idea of the children of Israel having a choice was not a new one; such freedom was given to our earliest ancestors. As a part of the consequences for Adam and Eve using that freedom to follow Satan, God told Adam,

> "The very ground is cursed because of you; getting food from the ground will be as painful as having babies is for your wife; you'll be working in pain all your life long. . . . Until you return to that ground yourself, dead and buried; you started out as dirt, you'll end up as dirt."[4]

The curse of dying applied to Adam and Eve and all of their descendants, including us, since we're all sinners.[5]

As a result of the tempter's role in deceiving humanity, God told him,

> "I will put enmity between you and the woman, and between your offspring and hers; he will crush your head, and you will strike his heel."[6]

This is the Bible's first prophecy of a savior to come into the world, Jesus Christ. His heel was wounded on the cross, but with His death and resurrection, Satan's head was crushed.

Though Satan now rules as the prince of the world,[7] this is a temporary situation. Satan and his followers are doomed to eternal destruction[8] via the "*second death*" described as "*the lake of fire*."[9] (emphasis mine) Joining the devil and his followers will be "the cowardly, the unbelieving, the vile, the murderers, the sexually immoral, those who practice magic arts, the idolaters and all liars."[10]

Theologians disagree as to whether the second death is a literal fire or a figurative way of saying that these souls have been removed from the presence of God completely. There is also debate as to whether hell represents an ongoing state of torment or the extinction of the soul as if this individual never had existed. The bottom line is that the second death is something we wish to avoid at all costs.

"The mind of sinful man is death."[11] The foregoing passage refers simultaneously to both the death of our bodies here on earth and the second death. The alternative to this destination is spelled out in the second part of the same verse, "But the mind controlled by the Spirit is life and peace."[12]

We make daily choices similar to those spelled out by Moses between God or god, life or death, light or darkness, being restored to a face-to-face relationship with our Creator in Heaven or following Satan to the second death.

While we will not avoid the death of our bodies, by making the right choices we can live at peace now as we anticipate that our souls will live forever with our Lord. The alternative is self-destruction and the second death by traveling the true highway to hell.

A vital question

What separates those sinners who are headed for the second death compared to others, also sinners, who will enjoy the face-to-face relationship with their Lord?

1. Even those earnestly seeking the Lord fall prey to forms of self-destruction including anger and resentment, stress, obsessive working, worry, over-eating, judging, greed—the list goes on and on. Further, everyone still will be in denial about some of these things when they die. Paul showed recognition of this in his own life when he wrote, "I do not understand what I do. For what I want to do I do not do but what I hate I do. . . . What a wretched man I am! Who will rescue me from this body of death?"[13]

He then answered his own question, "Thanks be to God—through Jesus Christ our Lord!"[14] He then wrote, "There is now no condemnation for those who are in Christ Jesus."[15]

In short, Christians are saved by grace.

2. Those on the highway to hell see the universe backward and suffer a complete black-out in their spiritual vision. They never seek the Lord and persist with a me-me-me perspective. Unless

they change their course, they will self-destruct blindly and join Satan in the second death. Their ultimate separation from God is an extension of their life on earth.

Hurting yourself

In my daily drunkenness, I was on a fast-track to self-destruction. Recall that I suffered from physical effects of drinking and seriously contemplated suicide.

Jesus dealt face-to-face with a man possessed by demons who was also on the fast-track and was in such anguish that he was mutilating himself. "Night and day among the tombs and in the hills he would cry out and cut himself with stones." When Jesus asked his name, the man replied, "My name is Legion. . .for we are many."[16] This shows that his very identity was determined by the demons that possessed him. Despite this, Jesus cast out the demons and healed this man.[17]

Still needing Jesus' healing are people today who self-mutilate like the demon-possessed man. This form of self-destruction was called the "the anorexia of the 1990s." A survey of college students found that 12 percent had harmed themselves intentionally. These people are called "cutters," but besides actually cutting themselves, they may burn themselves or bang their heads against a hard object. Why? According to an expert, "It reduces physiological and psychological attention" and has an immediate "calming effect" which they may describe as "numbing out."[18]

Think about this scenario. In order to help themselves, people self-destruct while hurting themselves. Their problem-solving skills are backward. Experts say that "cutters" often are motivated by a desire for control in their lives, but what they really need is God controlling their lives.

I, too, was seeking control through my false god of alcohol. You already know that I was in denial about the effects of my alcohol abuse, and it took a mental, physical, and spiritual toll on me. Like the "cutters" described above, I felt a need to be "numbed out."

Mentioned earlier was the parable of the lost son[19] whose self-destruction journey away from his father took him to the point where he wished he could line up with the pigs at feeding time. Jesus told this story to a predominantly Jewish audience who knew that under the Law of Moses, [20] they were forbidden not only to eat pork but couldn't even touch a pig. In hearing this story about a young man in the pig pen, the message was loud and clear that he had degenerated to the point where he was the scum of the earth. Such is the nature of self-destruction as we lose our identities of being made in the image of God.

Jesus said that everyone who sins is a slave to sin.[21] With my self-destructive past, it is easy for me to admit that I have been a slave to sin (and still am). What about you? In what way are you a slave to sin? Self-destructing?

It is more difficult to recognize this in ourselves if we've been going to church every Sunday and trying to do the right thing. Some routes to the far country, however, are more obscure than others.

The Rest of the Picture

Joseph Paul Franklin believed that God wanted him to start a race war. Between 1977 and 1980, he killed and wounded numerous people, mostly using a high-powered rifle from long distance. He is known as a "mission-oriented" serial killer; in each case, the victims were inter-racial couples or were connected somehow to the idea of what Franklin called "race-mixing." One shooting victim was *Hustler Magazine* publisher Larry Flynt, left paralyzed from the waist down, because he published pictures of an inter-racial couple in his magazine. Another victim was Vernon Jordan, leader of the National Urban League.

Franklin confessed to picking up two young white women who were hitch-hiking in West Virginia. He killed them both after one of them said she had a black boyfriend. "They told me they were into race-mixing. I just decided to waste 'em," Franklin later stated.[22]

From his cell on Missouri's death row, Franklin was interviewed by forensic psychologist Dr. Michael Weiner for a program shown on TruTV in 2008. In that interview, Franklin observed that his mission on earth had lasted three years, and then he added, the same duration of the earthly ministry of Jesus Christ.

"For you, Mr. Police. Call me God."[23]

So started a note found tacked to a tree outside a restaurant in

Ashland, Virginia, where a sniper had just wounded a man in October 2002. This was a part of what was known as the Beltway Sniper Attacks in which 10 people were killed and two more were wounded. The note contained a $10,000,000 ransom demand and warned that others would die if it was not heeded. Convicted in conjunction with these attacks were John Allen Muhammad and Lee Boyd Malvo.

South Korean student Cho Seung-Hui killed 32 people and wounded 25 others during his shooting rampage on the Virginia Tech campus in April 2007. He then took his own life.

Prior to the shootings, Seung-Hui made a videotape of himself and sent it to NBC news. In this tape, he said in part,

> "You thought it was one pathetic boy's life you were extinguishing. Thanks to you, I die like Jesus Christ, to inspire generations of the weak and defenseless people."[24]

What do these three accounts have in common? These murderers all made comparisons between themselves and deity. As a part of playing God and the distorted vision that goes with it, they justified taking the lives of others.

People who are self-destructing serve as destructive forces in the lives of others.

When asked about the greatest commandment, Jesus summarized the Ten Commandments while linking together an individual's relationship to God with his/her relationships with people.

> "'Love the Lord your God with all your heart and with all your soul and with all your mind.' This is the first and greatest commandment. And the second is like it: 'Love your neighbor as yourself.'"[25]

This demonstrates that our impact on the lives of others reflects our spiritual direction.

Douglas J. Rumford said it this way, "Whole people don't knowingly hurt people. Wounded people wound people."[26] Living in this fallen world, we are all wounded to one degree or another; we all have the capacity to serve as either positive or negative influences on the lives of others.

Paul wrote the following about people with "shameful lusts"[27] and those with "a depraved mind"[28] who assist Satan by giving approval to others on their way to destruction:

> "Although they know God's righteous decree that those who do such things deserve death, they not only continue to do these very things *but also approve of those who practice them.*"[29] (emphasis mine)

This is yet another way that one person guides another in self-destruction.

On the following pages are two biblical examples of the harm caused by self-destructing individuals.

We earlier discussed the married woman who committed adultery and was on a path of self-destruction.[30] There is also a warning about the results of having an affair with her.

> Keep to a path far from her,
> do not go near the door of her house,
> lest you give your best strength to others
> and your years to one who is cruel,
> lest strangers feast on your wealth
> and your toil enrich another man's house.
> At the end of your life you will groan,
> When your flesh and body are spent.
> You will say, "How I hated discipline!
> How my heart spurned correction!
> I would not obey my teachers
> or listen to my instructors.
> I have come to the brink of utter ruin
> in the midst of the assembly."[31]

We know that King David had an adulterous relationship with Bathsheba. It was harmful not only to him but to those around him. As a part of the cover-up, Bathsheba's husband, Uriah, and other soldiers died as innocent victims.[32]

Then later, the prophet Nathan, speaking for God, spelled out the consequences of David's actions. Not only would David be at war for the rest of his life,[33] but the infant born from his infidelity with Bathsheba would die.[34]

He also was told,

> "Out of your own household I am going to bring calamity upon you. Before your very eyes I will take your wives and give them to one who is close to you, and he will lie with your wives in broad daylight. You did it in secret, but I will do this in broad daylight before all Israel."[35]

As David heard this third consequence, he must have wondered how it would occur. It probably turned out uglier than he imagined. A sexual sin among David's children is detailed in II Samuel 12, immediately after the account of David and Bathsheba. The proximity of these stories communicates clearly that the activity of parents is monitored closely and mimicked by their children.

In this case, David's son Amnon was full of lust for his half-sister, Tamar. He set up a means to get Tamar by herself and raped her. The disgraced Tamar went to live with her full brother, Absalom, as "a desolate woman."[36] David was "furious"[37] but there is no record that he ever punished Amnon. Was this because he couldn't hold Amnon *to a higher sexual standard* than he had kept himself?

Two years later, Absalom told his servants to murder Amnon, and they did.[38] Absalom moved away for three years. David never punished Absalom. Was this because he couldn't hold Absalom *to a higher standard concerning murder* than he had kept himself?

Eventually, Absalom led a revolution to take over the kingdom from his father. David and his entourage had to evacuate Jerusalem before Absalom and his men entered. As prophesied, Absalom had sex on the roof of the palace with each of his father's concubines so that everyone in the kingdom would know about it.[39]

Absalom later was killed by his father's soldiers. "David was shaken. He went up to the room over the gateway and wept. As he went, he said: 'O my son Absalom! My son, my son Absalom! If only I had died instead of you—O Absalom, my son, my son!'"[40]

Weigh the choice of having a one-night stand with a married woman versus the consequences. David had the rest of his life to do that.

Everyday circumstances

In a moment of impatience, a mother or father can utter cross words that send lasting signals—or it may be a co-worker or friend who is on the receiving end of our wrath.

Due to our own spiritual problems, we may belittle or brow-beat others. There are plenty of other ways of projecting our own insecurities onto others, such as, "You'll never amount to anything" or "You're a trouble-maker, aren't you?" or "You're a mess. You never keep your room clean."

We may tell a person that he or she isn't __________ (pick a word, such as good/talented/smart/creative or choose your own word) enough to ______________. (You fill in the blank.) Who are we to say that this person can't do this? Do we think we're God?

It has been said that there is plenty of guilt to go around, and in some cases, people spread more than their fair share to the detriment of others.

The rolling of our eyes when someone else is talking or our inattentiveness send signals to other people that the things they have to say are either superfluous or not important. There are many different ways that body language communicates that we don't care.

The examples we set may send the wrong signals to loved ones, co-workers, even strangers. After all, a picture is worth a thousand words. Through our examples, what kind of messages are we sending?

Obviously, we do not have to be guilty of "black" sins to serve as a force of destruction in the lives of others.

Thus far, we've traced characteristics of Satan that show up in temptation and in the perspective of a person who has succumbed to temptation. In the chapters that follow, we'll see what it takes for a person to come out of denial and get off the road to self-destruction and on a journey toward Jesus.

ENDNOTES: CHAPTER NINE

1. http://en.wikipedia.org/wiki/Jerry_Garcia
2. Deuteronomy 30: 19-20.
3. Deuteronomy 30: 17-18.
4. Genesis 3: 17-19, *The Message.*
5. Romans 3: 23.
6. Genesis 3:15.
7. John 12: 31.
8. Matthew 25: 41; Revelation 20: 10.
9. Revelation 20: 14; 21:8.
10. Revelation 21: 8.
11. Romans 8: 6.
12. Romans 8: 6.
13. Romans 7: 15, 24.
14. Romans 7: 25.
15. Romans 8: 1.
16. Mark 5: 9.
17. Mark 5: 8, 11-15.
18. http://www.cyc-net.org/reference/refs-self-mutilation.html.
    http://www.focusas.com/SelfInjury.html
    http://www.fit.edu/caps/articles/documents/cutting.doc
19. Luke 15: 11-32.
20. Deuteronomy 14:8.
21. John 8: 34.
22. http://en.wikipedia.org/wiki/Joseph_Paul_Franklin
23. http://www.cbsnews.com/stories/2002/10/26/national/main527060.shtml?CMP=ILC-SearchStories
24. "Vengeful videos," *The Dallas Morning News*, April 19, 2007, p. 1-A.
25. Matthew 22: 37-39.
26. Douglas J. Rumford, *Questions God Asks, Questions Satan Asks*, Tyndale House Publishers, Inc., Wheaton, IL, 1998, p. 206.
27. Romans 1: 26.
28. Romans 1: 28.
29. Romans 1: 32.
30. Proverbs 5: 3-6.
31. Proverbs 5: 8-14.
32. II Samuel 11: 17.
33. II Samuel 12: 9-10.
34. II Samuel 12: 14.
35. II Samuel 12: 11-12.
36. II Samuel 13: 20.
37. II Samuel 13: 21.
38. II Samuel 13: 28-29.
39. II Samuel 16: 21-22.
40. II Samuel 18: 33.

Questions for Self-Examination and Group Discussion: Chapter 9

1. Name some messages you've observed in popular culture (television, movies, songs, etc.) that give the impression that the journey toward hell is a pleasant one.

2. Name some ways that demonstrate you understand the truth of Jesus's statement that everyone who sins is a slave to sin. If we are all sinners and therefore slaves to sin, does this mean that we are all in denial and that we are all self-destructing? Yes or no? Give some reasons to back up your answer.

3. This chapter discussed subtle forms of self-destruction. What are some of the less obvious forms of self-destruction that might be found in the life of someone who attends church regularly?

4. Ultimately, God has control. This means that control issues (such as trying to control the lives of others) are forms of playing God. Name some examples of control issues that lead to denial and self-destruction.

5. Each day, we are faced with numerous choices that demonstrate whether one is following God or god. Citing examples from each side of the ledger, give examples of such choices that you have made.

6. Ongoing denial leads to self-destruction. Based on observations you've made, how have you seen this to be true? Give examples of how it has been true in your own life.

7. A drunk driver crashes into a car, killing four members of a family. This is an example of me-me-me behavior that creates destruction in the life of others. What are some less obvious ways that individuals may harm others? Cite examples of how your own version of me-me-me has been detrimental to others.

Chapter Ten: A Moment of Clarity

I walked through the door of the mental hospital to admit myself, undoubtedly reeking from the Scotch whiskey I'd just gulped down in the parking lot.

When the door closed, I momentarily sensed that somewhere inside of me was a barely discernable light. Its dimness might be likened to a flashlight with the very weakest of batteries, yet it was not extinguished.

I seemed to gain a glimmer of hope from the light. Was this a message that my indwelling Holy Spirit had not been quenched totally? Or was it a product of my confusion, anxiety, and desperation? I still don't know for sure, but I did not give it any spiritual significance at the time.

From previous chapters, you know that my admittance to a mental hospital on November 6, 1973, was the culmination of a speedy downhill spiral toward self-destruction. This had started a decade earlier when alcohol became my false god during my senior year of high school.

Of course, I had no idea at the time that God would later use this—the worst day of my life—as my greatest asset.

Within a few minutes after entering, I went through an admitting process. I watched as someone wrote "acute depression" on my chart. It seemed like a gross over-simplification to use a two-word label to describe the totality of how horrible I felt.

I hadn't eaten anything that day and not much the day before. Though it was past the lunch hour, a lady working in the cafeteria gave me a tuna sandwich. I sat by myself at a table trying to eat it and was joined by an attractive woman about my age. This was my first contact with a fellow patient. She asked me why I was so sad. I can't remember what I told her. She looked completely normal and happy and told me she was being released within a few hours. I never saw her again.

Due to my overwhelming despair, there wasn't much else I could do except pace the hallways during the first few days. At night, I had dreams about pouring beers down my throat. Then as the immediate effects of the large quantities of alcohol started to subside, I became acquainted with the people around me.

I was surprised that the numerous patients in their late teens did not seem to identify with me or view me as a peer. Though I was 27, I still thought of myself as a teenager on the inside, sort of like Peter

Pan. (Although I did not know it then, I was on the right track, at least partially. My emotional maturity was probably at the level of a mid-adolescent.)

My associates in the hospital turned out to be in their 30s and 40s, the same age of the people with whom I'd been working in my career as a journalist. A fellow patient, "Ron," age 42 with graying hair and employed as a trash collector, soon became a good friend.

After four or five days, I was able to go outside the hospital for R.T. (recreational therapy) which included mostly touch football games on the hospital grounds and to O.T. (occupational therapy), located in a small, separate building. It was there that I made a ceramic ashtray and a leather-craft belt and did two oil paintings (by the numbers).

I also had time to contemplate what was going on in my life.

When I was kicked out of college for low grades at age 20, I had worked for several months in a geriatric unit at a large state mental hospital. The first time I entered that ward, the stench of bodily waste made me nauseous.

The average person hardly could fathom the sad state of humanity residing behind the locked doors of that state institution. Most of the patients had no chance of ever going home. Many of them operated on what might be described as a sub-human level. On one occasion, for instance, I saw a man named Ben get down on his knees and put his face into the toilet bowl to get a drink of water. A water fountain was a few feet away.

The hospital where I was a patient was private and expensive. In many, many ways, it was far removed from the state hospital where I had worked. It occurred to me that if the course of my life did not change, the next stop on my downward path would be in a hospital like the one where I had worked earlier. My life would be wasted!

I also began to realize that I wasn't Peter Pan. I had harbored some vague notions that in my boyishness, I really was not responsible for my actions. I had deluded myself in thinking that any bad thing I did somehow could be taken back. It began to dawn on me that I was an adult and my actions might be irrevocable. Before I left the hospital, I knew I was playing for all the marbles.

The previous year's diagnosis of an enlarged liver from drinking hadn't accomplished this, but all the mental anguish finally landing me in a mental hospital caused me take a good look in the mirror. During these periods of self-examination, the dark veil of denial was partially lifted. This was my moment of clarity. I started to get a picture of the self-destructive road I was traveling.

A moment of clarity may serve to shatter the foundations of denial.

The lost son from Jesus' parable[1] had his moment of clarity while employed in a pig pen. "He longed to fill his stomach with the pods that the pigs were eating, but no one gave him anything. When he came to his senses"[2] and examined his position in life, he realized he was starving to death.[3]

The words "When he came to his senses"[4] tell the story. The *King James Version* of the Bible makes a parallel point in its translation of this same phrase, "And when he came to himself."

In Chapter 8, we mentioned that Saul (later called Paul) had it backward because as a religious man, he thought he was doing a Godly service by persecuting Christians.[5] He also had a moment of clarity after he was struck blind by a light from heaven and heard the voice of Jesus.

> Saul got up from the ground, but when he opened his eyes he could see nothing. So they led him by the hand into Damascus. For three days he was blind, and did not eat or drink anything.[6]

Put yourself in Saul's shoes. You're 100% certain that you are doing the right thing by persecuting Christians. Then suddenly, a bright light appears; Jesus calls you by name and says you've been persecuting Him. He tells you to go into the city and await word on what to do next.

Would this get your attention? Would you wonder whether you'd be blind for the rest of your life? Could you have been absolutely wrong about Jesus Christ? Is it possible that while you thought you had spiritual clarity, you actually were spiritually blind?

After three days of sightlessness, not eating or drinking and undoubtedly a great deal of self-examination, would you be ready for some answers?

Seeking a new direction

The moment of clarity may lead people to conclude that they should change their path in life. They may seek new information rather than justify the same old lifestyle in the same old manner. They then may act on this new information.

When Saul was ready, the Lord sent Ananias as a messenger. If Ananias had come three and a half days earlier, he would have been sent straight to the slammer. Saul was all ears, however, when the Lord's messenger did show up.

> Placing his hands on Saul, he said, "Brother Saul, the Lord—Jesus, who appeared to you on the road as you were coming here—has sent me so that you may see again and be filled with the Holy Spirit." Immediately, something like scales fell from Saul's eyes, and he could see again. He got up and was baptized, and after taking some food, he regained his strength.[7]

With the information provided by Ananias and a moment of clarity both spiritually and visually, Saul took immediate action. Even before eating, he was baptized into Christ. Soon, Saul was preaching "That Jesus Christ is the son of God."[8] He went on to become the most prominent New Testament author.

What a huge turn-around in his life!

In the case of the lost son, his moment of clarity got him thinking about how good he'd had it at home. "How many of my father's hired men have food to spare, and here I am starving to death!" With that in mind, he said to himself, "I will set out and go back to my father."[9]

Don't miss this: With the blinders of denial lifted, the son started thinking differently about his father. This father wasn't the old fuddy-duddy who was out to prevent him from having a good time, as per his conjured murky perspective. This was a father who'd always loved him and wanted the best for him. The son then headed in the direction of home.

Like Saul/Paul, when I was ready to hear the truth, God sent a messenger. In my case, it was my fellow patient, Ron.

I can't remember what prompted this, perhaps it was our previous conversations, but one day he pulled out a questionnaire about drinking. Would I like to answer the questions? Sure, I replied. They went something like this: "Have you ever had a morning drink?" "Have there been periods while drinking when you were not able to remember what happened the night before?" "Have you ever missed work because of drinking?" There were 44 in all.

I answered yes to 41 of the questions and thought that someone would have to answer affirmatively to all of them to be a problem drinker. Imagine my surprise, then, when Ron read the key at the end: "If you answered yes to two of these, you have a serious drinking problem. If you answered yes to three or more, you are an alcoholic."

Hmmmm.

It seems incredible, but this was my first indication from a source with expertise (the questionnaire developed by a prestigious university) that I was an alcoholic. Once, I had mentioned the extent of my drinking to a psychologist I started seeing for anxiety problems a few months after starting newspaper work. He dismissed the idea. In fact, the psychologist and I imbibed together on a few occasions. He also encouraged me to smoke marijuana. The psychologist's idea seemed to be that alcohol was a temporary means for me to get by while he helped me delve into the real root of my problems; if I understood the nature of my problems, my drinking would level off. I subsequently found out that no amount of self-awareness would alleviate a drinking problem like mine.

In the hospital, I was seeing a psychiatrist every other day, and he never asked about my drinking habits. After taking the questionnaire with Ron, I asked this doctor if I might be an alcoholic. "Maybe," he replied, and that was about as far as the discussion went.

Ron and I started sharing drinking stories. His booze intake resulted in his being admitted to the hospital on the verge of delirium tremens. His aging mother had forked over her life savings to pay for his stay there. She'd been a heavy drinker earlier in her life but had been sober more than 20 years through her membership in a group that helped problem drinkers. Ron planned to join this organization as soon as he left the hospital.

He recommended that I try it, too.

Hmmmm, again.

My veil of denial had been lifted but not completely. At this point, I still did not connect my mental problems with my drinking, but I could see that the booze was not helping me. I did not know if the organization he recommended would be of benefit, but I was willing to try it.

Ron and I both vowed that upon leaving the hospital, we would try not to drink. Further, we both planned to attend meetings of the group for problem drinkers. I carried these ideas with me when due to financial concerns, I checked out of the hospital after two weeks.

I had grave trepidations about leaving the safe confines of the hospital but knew that the problems I needed to face were in the real world. I now can say with certainty that Ron had given me the information I needed to embark on a new life.

My self-examination and the moment of clarity that followed helped set the stage for trying something different.

What's needed to end denial

I know of three things that serve to guide an individual in having a moment of clarity:

1. Discomfort

For some people, life becomes so painful, and the prospects for the future are so dim, it becomes obvious that they need to do something different. This was the case with the lost son and with me. Similarly, the blinded Saul had to come to grips with the painful fact that his life was a lie. As a result, we all had our moments of clarity.

Other instances may be found in the Bible.

For example, how would you like to be led around by a hook that was stuck through your nose? This pain and humiliation caused a turn-around in the life of Manasseh, king of Judah starting in 687 B.C.[10] Here is the biblical account:

> The Lord spoke to Manasseh and his people, but they paid no attention. So the Lord brought against them the army commanders of the king of Assyria, who took Manasseh prisoner, put a hook in his nose, bound him with bronze shackles and took him to Babylon. In his distress he sought the favor of the Lord his God and humbled himself greatly before the God of his fathers. And when he prayed to him, the Lord was moved by his entreaty and listened to his plea; so he brought him back to Jerusalem and to his kingdom. Then Manasseh knew that the Lord is God.[11]

Apparently, Manasseh was able to see past the hook for his moment of clarity. Undoubtedly, though, there are individuals who continue in denial and discomfort and either do not heed their moment or never have it.

There also are those who have moments of clarity, apparently take note of them, but subsequently fall back to their old ways. Perhaps, they are described in Jesus' Parable of the Sower[12] as the seed that fell among the rocks or thorns—or they are like the children of Israel who wanted to return to slavery rather than go on to the Promised Land.

Unfortunately, Ron was a case in point. He left the mental hospital a few weeks after I did. Since we lived quite a distance apart, we did not see each other face to face but talked on the telephone several times. For a while, he stayed off booze and attended recovery group meetings. The last time we talked, he reported that too many people at the recovery group in his town used bad language so he decided not to go anymore. (It's not as though he never had used this language himself, though.) One afternoon a few weeks later, I called, and his mother answered. She said Ron had come home drunk and was in bed asleep.

He and I lost touch after that, so I don't know whether he was able to sober up again or continued toward self-destruction. I'll always be grateful to him for bringing me the message I needed to hear.

2. Intervention

A moment of clarity may occur when someone confronts a person in denial about his/her self-destructive path. Borrowing from addiction-recovery language, I refer to this as an intervention.

An intervention may or may not be heeded. Steve Steele, a friend of mine who works in a Christian addiction recovery ministry, directed interventions on two men with whom I was well acquainted; both had strong church backgrounds and were killing themselves with booze. One of these men now leads a sober, productive life, and the other died as a direct result of his alcoholism.

The concept of an intervention may be found in both the Old and New Testaments.

As an example, Jesus said, "If your brother sins against you, go and show him his fault, just between the two of you."[13] If the person does not listen, the Lord said to go again, this time taking two or three others.[14]

> "If he still won't listen, tell the church. If he won't listen to the church, you'll have to start over from scratch, confront him with the need for repentance, and offer again God's forgiving love."[15]

The idea is to lead the person to a moment of clarity so that he/she may understand the wrong committed and be restored as a brother or sister. (Be cautious, though—our feelings of being sinned against often are manifestations of me-me-me.)

The Lord led Nathan the Prophet to an intervention on King David after his adultery with Bathsheba.[16] Since a baby had been born, David had continued in denial for at least nine months.[17]

Initially, Nathan told David a story about two men who lived in the same town. One of them had one female lamb that he and his children loved and treated as a family member. The second was a rich man with many sheep and cattle. This man killed the one precious lamb owned by his neighbor and prepared it as a meal for a guest in his home.[18]

> David burned with anger against the man and said to Nathan, "As surely as the Lord lives, the man who did this deserves to die! He must pay for that lamb four times over, because he did such a thing and had no pity."[19]

"Then Nathan said to David, 'You are the man!'"[20] Nathan went on to detail many of the Lord's blessings received by David, the wrongs committed by David, and the consequences he would face as a result of them.

Finally, David had a moment of clarity and said, "I have sinned against the Lord."[21]

At least, David finally heeded the prophet and came out of denial. Selecting to stay in denial was King Amaziah, ruler of Judah from 796 to 767 B.C. [22]

Amaziah returned from a military victory carrying some idols from the people he'd conquered and worshipped them as his false gods. The Lord sent a prophet to the king who asked, "Why do you consult this people's gods, which could not save their own people from your hand?"[23]

Amaziah cut him off. "Have we appointed you an adviser to the king? Stop! Why be struck down?"[24]

Rather than setting things right, Amaziah continued in denial toward self-destruction, which included a military defeat, the loss of the riches in the temple of God in Jerusalem, and his eventual murder.[25]

As demonstrated by Amaziah, people sometimes blame the

messenger. Another such instance included Hanani, the seer, who was thrown in jail after taking a message of the Lord to King Asa, ruler of Judah from 911-870 B.C.[26]

The prophet Daniel did an intervention as a part of interpreting a dream for Nebuchadnezzar, king of Babylon.[27] After the king reported details of the dream, Daniel told him, in short, that he would go insane if he continued on the same arrogant path. Daniel concluded with this advice:

> "Renounce your sins by doing what is right, and your wickedness by being kind to the oppressed. It may be that then your prosperity will continue."[28]

Perhaps, the king heeded this message for a while, but a year later, Nebuchadnezzar stood on the roof of his palace and said, "Is not this the great Babylon I have built as the royal residence, by my mighty power and for the glory of my majesty?"[29] That sentence reeks of me-me-me and the worship of self as a false god.

If this had occurred some 2,500 years later, the king might have joined Ron's and my looping together leather-craft belts in occupational therapy. Instead, here is what happened:

> The words were still on his lips when a voice came from heaven, "This is what is decreed for you, King Nebuchadnezzar: Your royal authority has been taken from you. You will be driven away from people and will

> live with the wild animals; you will eat grass like cattle. Seven times will pass by for you until you acknowledge that the Most High is sovereign over the kingdoms of men and gives them to anyone he wishes."[30]

I'm not sure what it is like to go through something like this, but we may conclude that it was an experience Nebuchadnezzar did not wish to repeat. Here's what he said about it,

> "At the end of that time, I, Nebuchadnezzar, raised my eyes toward heaven, and my sanity was restored. Then I praised the Most High; I honored and glorified him who lives forever."[31]

The king's story contains both an intervention and discomfort. That's what it took for him to understand the folly of playing God.

3. Self-examination

Both discomfort or intervention may lead to self-examination that is followed by a moment of clarity, but neither are necessary prerequisites to self-examination. Among spiritually mature Christians, ongoing self-examination may become nearly reflexive as these individuals continually compare themselves to Jesus Christ. When falling short, these Christians often may know about it quite quickly, as self-examination prompts a moment of clarity.

The self-examination may occur at any time of any day of the week, but a special time for it is when Christians take communion as described below:

> Whoever eats the bread or drinks the cup of the Lord in an unworthy manner will be guilty of sinning against the body and blood of the Lord. A man ought to examine himself before he eats of the bread and drinks of the cup. For anyone who eats and drinks without recognizing the body of the Lord eats and drinks judgment on himself.[32]

Who is the person who eats and drinks unworthily? The individual who does not go through a self-examination process and make a comparison between self and Jesus. By comparing self to Jesus, Christians know why he died for them.

As described above, a moment of clarity is related to the end of denial. This denial may affect the overall direction of one's life, such as it did with the Saul/Paul, the lost son, and me—or the moment of clarity may serve to guide a spiritually mature person in making small but needed corrections. In the course of one's lifetime, it may be possible to experience moments of clarity by the hundreds that vary in magnitude.

The next chapter addresses what follows a moment of clarity.

Endnotes: Chapter 10

1. Luke 15: 11-32.
2. Luke 15: 16-17.
3. Luke 15: 17.
4. Luke 15: 17.
5. Acts 9: 1-2.
6. Acts 9: 8-9.
7. Acts 9: 17-19.
8. Acts 9: 20.
9. Luke 15: 17-18
10. J. D. Douglas and Merrill C. Tenney (Editors), *The New International Dictionary of the Bible*, Zondervan Publishing House, Grand Rapids, MI, 1987, p. 618.
11. II Chronicles 33: 10-13.
12. Matthew 13: 3-9; 18-23.
13. Matthew 18: 15.
14. Matthew 18: 16.
15. Matthew 18: 17, *The Message.*
16. II Samuel 12: 1-12.
17. II Samuel 11: 27.
18. II Samuel 12: 1-4.
19. II Samuel 12: 5-6.
20. II Samuel 12: 7.
21. II Samuel 12: 13.
22. Henry Hampton Halley, *Halley's Bible Handbook with the new International Version*, Zondervan Publishing House, Grand Rapids, MI, 2000, p. 281.
23. II Chronicles 25: 15.
24. II Chronicles 25: 16.
25. II Chronicles 25.
26. Henry Hampton Halley, *op cit.*, p. 279; II Chronicles 16.
27. Daniel 4.
28. Daniel 4: 27.
29. Daniel 4: 30.
30. Daniel 4: 31-32.
31. Daniel 4: 34.
32. I Corinthians 11: 27-29.

Questions for Self-Examination and Group Discussion: Chapter 10

1. Describe how self-examination and the moment of clarity are connected to the end of denial.

2. The phrases "And when he came to himself" and "When he came to his senses" are both used to describe what occurred when the lost son had a moment of clarity in the pig pen. Describe what these two phrases mean in terms of the lost son described in Luke 15: 11-28, in terms of anyone coming out of denial.

3. After his moment of clarity, the lost son started thinking differently about his father. How does denial affect the way people perceive God? What might occur in someone's life for that person to start thinking of God with greater clarity?

4. Why do people sometimes strike out at a person sent to bring them some information they need? Name some instances that were described in the New Testament where people struck out at Jesus Christ for telling them the truth.

5. The Lord sent Ananias to Saul when he was ready to hear a new message. Ron served as the author's messenger. Name some messengers that have come into your life at important times, and relate how your life was changed as a result. Would you always have been receptive to these messengers? Why or why not?

6. Name some moments of clarity you've experienced that have opened the door to a new look at yourself. How did these moments of clarity affect your relationship with God?

7. Give examples of when discomfort and/or an intervention caused you to examine yourself anew. What were you in denial about? In what way is self-examination in comparison to Jesus a part of your life today?

Chapter Eleven:

Repentance and Confession

A few days after leaving the mental hospital, I drove with great trepidation to my first meeting for problem drinkers. Upon arrival, I was welcomed by eight or 10 men sitting around a table drinking coffee.

Once the meeting started, a member who was a physician said I was the most important person there. Wow, I thought. Then he added, "Because you remind us of the way we were when we first got here." Was this good or bad? I wasn't sure, but my overall impression was very positive.

Before the meeting was over, someone wrote on a paper napkin, "Before you take the first drink, call me." Everyone present signed his name and added his telephone number before I was given the napkin. This marked the beginning of the end of the isolation I'd been feeling for years. I carried that napkin in my wallet for a long time thereafter.

In the weeks that followed, I learned that members of this group refer to their program as spiritual but not religious. Although I didn't know the difference, I was glad to hear that God was involved. I had little faith in my professed atheism and secretly had harbored thoughts of returning to church some day.

Odd as this may seem, I didn't identify immediately when people said they wanted to stop drinking. I wanted to live without the overwhelming hangovers, anxieties, and fears of impending doom. I still hadn't shaken completely the idea that alcohol was providing a temporary means of dealing with my mental illness. Despite this, I vowed to continue with the non-drinking pact with Ron from the hospital.

Members of the group kept referring to "the 12 steps" as guiding principles for contentment and sobriety.[1] The first step is "We admitted we were powerless over alcohol, that our lives had become unmanageable."

By listening to others talk about this step, I finally saw the light. Alcohol was the problem and not the solution as I had long thought—the beer and booze were causing the anxieties, not curing them. As an alcoholic, I had lost the ability to be a social drinker. The first drink immediately would get me back on the road to daily drunkenness. Complete abstinence from alcohol was my only solution.

This was a huge leap forward as the truth finally trumped out the lie to which I had subscribed for the past decade. Additionally, I had thought of myself as a victim of mental illness, and I had no idea how to alleviate the problem. By defining myself as an alcoholic, there was something positive I could do on my own behalf—not pick up the first drink.

In order to reach a solution, it is important to recognize the true nature of the problem, and that is what Step One did for me.

I also found that the longer I stayed sober, the fewer anxieties I experienced. I was assured by other group members that things would keep getting better.

In the previous chapter, I wrote that the veil of denial was lifted partially by my moment of clarity in the hospital. Taking Step One lifted that veil considerably higher. The steps that followed dealt with my relationships with both God and people, the very same concerns expressed in the Ten Commandments and the "Big Two" itemized by Jesus as loving God with all my heart and loving my neighbor as myself.[2]

If it sounds like this spiritual program is based on biblical principles, you are correct. For example, I was told that I did not have to go the rest of my life without drinking; all I had to do was not take a drink today. This is based on Jesus' words from the Sermon on the Mount, "Therefore do not worry about tomorrow, for tomorrow will worry about itself. Each day has enough trouble of its own."[3]

Back to church

After a few months of learning about sobriety and spirituality, I started thinking about returning to church. I prayed about it. Then on three consecutive Sundays, I visited a neighborhood congregation of the religious group in which I had grown up. No one talked to me—not even when I tried to initiate it. Surely, I reasoned, it was not God's will for me to attend such a church, and I never returned.

I continued to pray and settled in my mind that I would go anywhere God sent me. A few days later, my mother called and said I had received an invitation to a church that was hosting a reunion for former students of the Christian college from which I had graduated four and a half years earlier. It was several miles away, but I went and enjoyed the reunion.

As I was leaving, I was approached by the minister and his wife. They asked me where I attended church.

"No where," I replied. Then I told them about my recent stay in the mental hospital and my alcoholism.

"We could use someone like you around here," said the minister. He didn't seem to be joking. With the way I'd been living, I felt very unworthy about showing up in church. The congregation where no one talked to me only reinforced this, but this minister's positive approach helped to alleviate that concern. I took this as the answer to my prayer and started attending services there. I was welcomed warmly.

In the months that followed, I could be found each day at a recovery group meeting, church, or both. At the recovery group meetings, I was told that my sobriety was contingent upon my spiritual condition. I believed this because I saw it to be true in the lives of others.

My murky spiritual vision was clearing little by little. Down the street from the church was the place where I had seen the blooming flowers in May 1974 and had known I was looking at the world differently.

Around the same time, I started to get some ideas about the ramifications of turning my back on God, daily drunkenness, and my relationships with other people during that time. It became clear that I had been wrong about many things. This kind of self-assessment was new to me. In my denial, I previously had justified all of my actions while avoiding personal responsibility for them. I was undergoing a process of *repentance*, although I would not have labeled it as such at the time.

> Repentance is a profound change of mind involving the changing of the direction of life from that of self-centeredness or sin-centeredness to God or Christ-centeredness.[4]

At first, I recognized only the most blatant activities from my past, such as getting drunk and smashing some windows. As my understanding of God's will continued to grow, however, I had ongoing moments of clarity in regard to probably hundreds of episodes from my self-centered past. This continued even after many years of sobriety. It is likened to the unpeeling of an onion with multiple layers, both thick and thin. I repented of the types of thoughts and behaviors I hoped not to repeat.

Still continuing on this journey today, most of my moments of clarity and repentance deal with my self-centered *present*.

As Paul wrote, "Godly sorrow brings repentance. . .and leaves no regret."[5]

Total repentance?

John Paul Franklin was named in Chapter 9 as a man who compared himself to Jesus Christ and murdered others for "race mixing" between 1977 and 1980.

A 1990 story in the *New York Times* commemorated the ten-year anniversary of the deaths of Ted Fields, 20, and David Martin, 18, both black men shot by sniper fire as they were jogging with white women in Salt Lake City, Utah. Franklin confessed to these killings in a television interview. "Had they not been race mixing, you know, it would have been a totally different story," Franklin told the reporter.

The story continued: "Although he said he spends most of his time in his cell reading the Bible and praying, Mr. Franklin had no remorse for the Utah murders and expressed white supremacist views."

> "No, I don't regret that," he said of the slayings. "Not to say there are not actions that I've done that I don't regret. I've sinned a lot in my life. Any sins that I've done I've repented of."[6]

Talk about denial and blind spots! Though Franklin's are more blatant than most, denial and blind spots are common to all of us. Spiritually maturing people recognize the importance of repentance.

Even the most spiritually advanced individuals, however, will not have repented of all their sins when they meet their Creator face to face. At that moment, we'll all have a better understanding of the depth of the grace granted us through Jesus.

The idea of repentance is found throughout the Old Testament.[7]

In the New Testament, both John the Baptist and Peter preached repentance in conjunction with baptism.[8] Addressing some Greek intellectuals, Paul referred to man-made idols, then stated, "In the past God over-looked such ignorance, but now he commands all people everywhere to repent."[9]

The scope of this book coincides with what Paul wrote to Timothy,

> God's servant must not be argumentative, but a gentle listener and a teacher who keeps cool, working firmly but patiently with those who refuse to obey. You never know how or when God might sober them up with a change of heart and a turning to the truth, enabling them to escape the Devil's trap, where they are caught and held captive, forced to run his errands.[10]

Confession

Kim and I attend a church in Dallas, Texas, that usually has somewhere between 1,500 and 2,000 worshippers on Sunday morning. There are many people I know only by sight, not by name. One such person was Charlie Reed.

In early 2003, our minister hosted a series for men that ran for several consecutive Saturday mornings. One day, I arrived after the lesson already had started and sat next to a friend near the back row. Charlie was sitting on the other side of my friend.

Toward the end of the session, the minister told us to select a man sitting near us to confess a spiritual shortcoming. By this time, our mutual friend had left, so Charlie and I slid together and introduced ourselves. He then expressed a concern that was very bothersome to him in his Christian walk. When he was finished, I said, "That's a big problem for me, too." We talked about this topic for the next few minutes. Then the day's activities were over.

After that, I would wave to Charlie or say hello, but we never had another conversation. About a year and a half later, Charlie, age 40, was found dead in his pick-up truck. The engine was running, and the air conditioner was turned to full blast. Apparently, he had felt overheated while working in hot weather and had gotten into the truck to cool off, and his heart gave out. Though he'd recently undergone a thorough physical, Charlie never knew that he had a so-called "widow-maker" blockage in his heart. This was discovered in his autopsy.

Several months later, his widow, Sharon, approached me. She related a conversation she'd had with Charlie about how much I'd meant to him and how much he appreciated my friendship.

Remember, our relationship was based on one conversation that lasted about five minutes. The important thing was not the duration but the quality of what occurred.

As Christians, we are admonished to "Carry each other's burdens."[11] This is exactly what went on between Charlie and me.

Who benefited? We both did. For those few minutes, we made ourselves transparent to each other, and the isolation we each felt as a result of this mutual difficulty was gone.

Does the statement about the end of isolation sound familiar? As a reminder, this is the same description I used earlier in this chapter after I attended my first meeting for problem drinkers.

A brief digression

As I write these words on my laptop, it is a rainy Friday morning in Dallas. On Monday night of this week, I attended a Christian recovery group that meets weekly and is chaired by Steve Steele, my friend mentioned earlier. About 20 people were in attendance, including a man in his 40s, Keith, who's had a terrible time with addictions to sex, drugs, and alcohol. Due to God's grace, he is doing much better now. His parents, long-time Christians, sat next to him. It was their first time at an addiction recovery meeting.

Last night, Keith sat next to me at a men's meeting I chaired at my own church. I asked what his parents thought about Monday's session. He answered, "After it was over, my dad went to Steve and told him, 'This is the way things should be at church.'"

"I've heard that a thousand times," Steve replied.

I have, too. Having attended both church and recovery group meetings for many years, I believe this is absolutely valid.

Like others, I openly confess shortcomings at just about every recovery group meeting I attend. Beside that, Step Four includes a written moral inventory of our pasts, and Step Five has us confessing these things to God, to ourselves, and another human being.

My fourth step filled seventy hand-written pages in a spiral binder. Then I sat down with a trusted friend and went through it as a part of Step Five. When it was over, I burned the notebook in a fire, and all that was left was the spiral.

There are provisions in Steps Eight and Nine for recognizing individuals we harmed in the past and making amends to them. The tenth step includes ongoing self-examination and making things right.

People in recovery groups do a lot of self-examination, repentance, and confession, and this process becomes a part of their very natures.

In September 1974, when I had about 10 months of sobriety, I "went forward" at church during what we call the invitation song that follows the sermon. Some people would refer to this as an altar call. I had been baptized at age 11, so I did not believe that necessary. My purpose was to be restored to the Lord's body by telling of my repentance. In other words, I confessed to them.

Outside of responding to an invitation, there is no other formal means of confession in the churches I've attended. It is possible, though, that confession goes on in small groups and between Christian friends.

What I've usually found, however, is that people at church are hush-hush in regard to what's really going on in their lives. Sure, we pray for those who are physically ill, but there's not much prayer about people who suffer from spiritual illnesses. It's as if we don't want

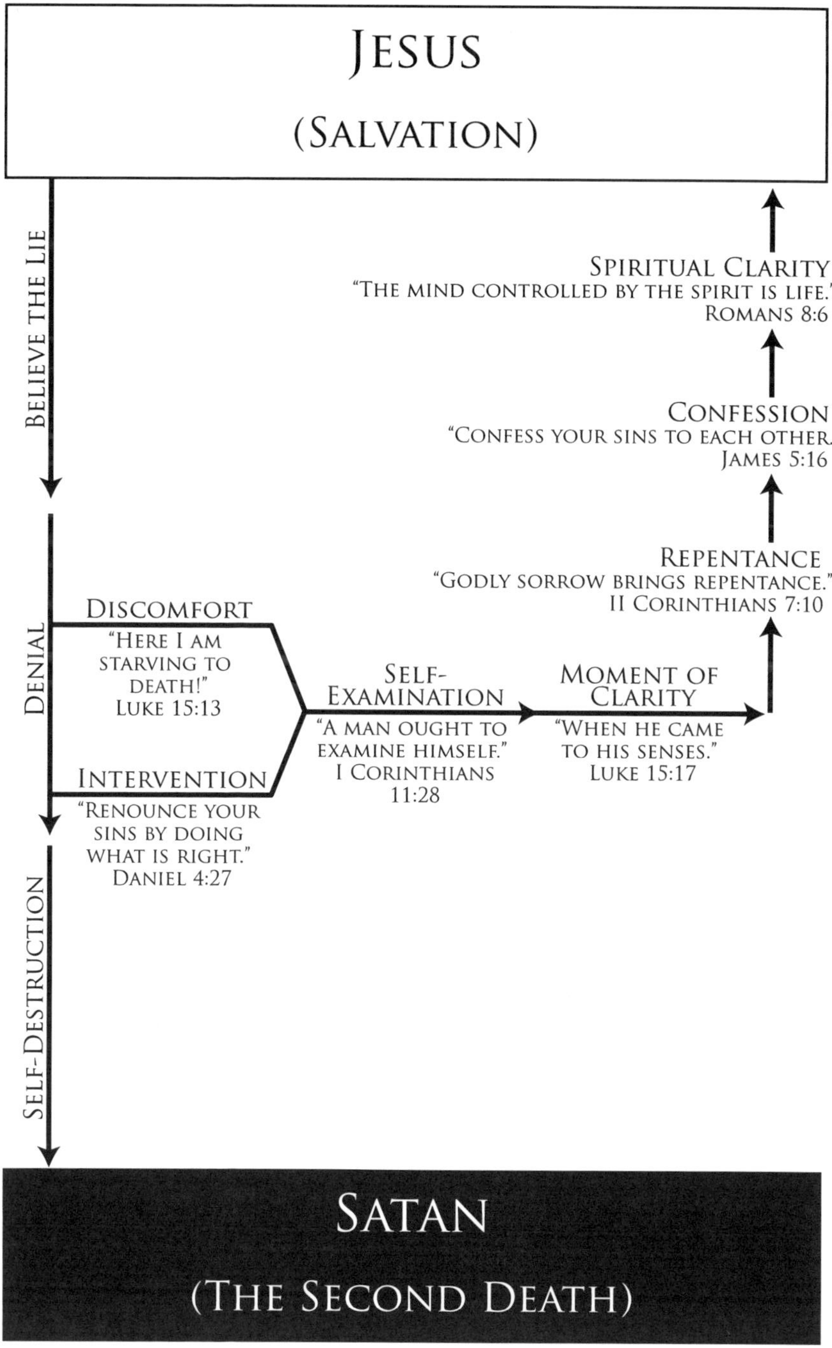
JESUS
(SALVATION)
BELIEVE THE LIE
DENIAL
SELF-DESTRUCTION
SPIRITUAL CLARITY
"THE MIND CONTROLLED BY THE SPIRIT IS LIFE."
ROMANS 8:6
CONFESSION
"CONFESS YOUR SINS TO EACH OTHER."
JAMES 5:16
REPENTANCE
"GODLY SORROW BRINGS REPENTANCE."
II CORINTHIANS 7:10
DISCOMFORT
"HERE I AM STARVING TO DEATH!"
LUKE 15:13
INTERVENTION
"RENOUNCE YOUR SINS BY DOING WHAT IS RIGHT."
DANIEL 4:27
SELF-EXAMINATION
"A MAN OUGHT TO EXAMINE HIMSELF."
I CORINTHIANS 11:28
MOMENT OF CLARITY
"WHEN HE CAME TO HIS SENSES."
LUKE 15:17
SATAN
(THE SECOND DEATH)

others at church to know that we have problems.

Sometimes, people at church have responded to the invitation and then confessed to having sinned or to being a sinner. Such an admission is parallel to someone confessing that they need air to breathe. This is because sinning is common to everyone.

Remember, I really couldn't get on the road to spiritual recovery until I took Step One and admitted to myself and others what really was wrong with me: I'm an alcoholic. It is important to put the right names on things when we are confessing.

Paul wrote this to the church at Corinth,

> Neither the sexually immoral nor idolaters nor adulterers nor male prostitutes nor homosexual offenders nor thieves nor the greedy nor drunkards nor slanderers nor swindlers will inherit the kingdom of God.[12]

Then Paul added, "And that is what some of you were."[13]

How did Paul know that some of those people being saved by grace had been guilty of various sexual sins, drunkenness, etc.? Don't you think that these people confessed these things after they had repented?

James wrote, "Confess your sins to each other and pray for each other so that you may be healed."[14]

If we don't confess the exact nature of our sins, we will live in isolation, and our fellow Christians won't be able to help us bear our burdens because they won't know about them.

> If we claim to be without sin, we deceive ourselves and the truth is not in us. If we confess our sins, he is faithful and just and will forgive us our sins and purify us from all unrighteousness. If we claim we have not sinned, we make him out to be a liar and his word has no place in our lives.[15]

Endnotes: Chapter Eleven

1. Based on biblical principles used by the Oxford Group in the 1920s, the 12 steps to recovery were written by members of Alcoholics Anonymous shortly after the establishment of that group in the late 1930s. The same 12 steps are used today by some 200 different programs to overcome a wide variety of spiritually based problems. For more information on the steps and their biblical basis, see Don Umphrey, *12 Steps to a Closer Walk with God: A Guide for Small Groups*, Third Edition, Quarry Press, Dallas, Texas, 2004.
2. Matthew 22: 37-39.
3. Matthew 6: 34.
4. J. D. Douglas and Merrill C. Tenney, *The New International Dictionary of the Bible*, Zondervan Publishing House, Grand Rapids, MI, 1987, p. 853.
5. II Corinthians 7: 10.
6. http://query.nytimes.com/gst/fullpage.html?res=9C0CE7DF113DF932A1575BC0A966958260
7. II Kings 17: 13; Isa. 19:22; Jer. 3:12, 14, 22; Jonah 3: 10.
8. Matthew 3: 2, 8; Acts 2: 38.
9. Acts 17: 30.
10. II Timothy 2: 24-26, *The Message.*
11. Galatians 6: 2.
12. I Corinthians 6: 9-10.
13. I Corinthians 6: 11.
14. James 5: 16.
15. I John 1: 8-10.
16. J. D. Douglas and Merrill C. Tenney, *op cit.*, p. 853.

Questions for Self-Examination and Group Discussion: Chapter 11

1. What is the relationship between denial and both repentance and confession?

2. The same authors who wrote that definition of repentance used in this chapter followed it with this statement, "God's forgiveness is available only to those who are repentant, for only they can receive it."[16] Do you believe this to be true? Why or why not?

3. The author stated that the veil of denial was lifted even further because he took the first step and put the true label on what really was wrong with him. What are the advantages of confessing the true nature of our wrongs rather than a more vague confession of being a sinner?

4. Contrast the effect on the author of visiting the church where no one talked with him compared to the church where the minister said they could use someone like him. Share some experiences from your own life where you were rejected, compared to, accepted. Have these experiences guided the way you treat other people? If yes, how?

5. Thinking about the definition of repentance used in this chapter, what are some things of which you have repented previously. Did you confess them to God? To another human being? How has confessing or not confessing to God affected you? How has confessing or not confessing to another human being affected you?

6. Describe how your veil of denial has been lifted by recent moments of clarity in your own life. Have you repented of these things?

7. Following the example of confession between Charlie and the author, select another person to confess some spiritual shortcomings that have been bothering you—and listen while the other person confesses to you.

Chapter Twelve: Humility and Pride

When I was a junior in high school, my American History teacher was a big, burly man and very demonstrative. His size added emphasis to his sweeping gestures. Sometimes he would sweat and wipe his face with his handkerchief. In doing this one day, something originating in his nose was transferred inadvertently to his cheek. It stuck there, and everyone in the room could see it but him.

Every time I looked in his direction, all I could think about was the offending object. This made paying attention to his words almost impossible. So I mostly looked down and tried to pretend that he was a radio.

I wanted so badly to raise my hand and tell him the obvious, but it was too embarrassing. Probably, others thought the same thing. How exactly would a 16-year-old student phrase such a statement to the teacher with the rest of the class listening? It was torture sitting there the next 25 or 30 minutes until the bell rang.

I've since wondered what it was like from his perspective. I'm pretty sure that starting at that one particular moment, none of the students made much eye contact with him. Did he wonder why? Did a fellow faculty member clue him in before the next class entered? I'll never know, but I can say that the problem was no longer present when I arrived at class the following day.

I was prompted to think about that incident by the story line of a poem written in 1786. It, too, was based on an actual occurrence. Here it is:

A young woman slid into a church pew on a Sunday morning. Her new hat represented the latest fashion statement, and she was confident that people sitting around her would be impressed accordingly.

When the worship service started, her expectations seemed to come to fruition. She was, indeed, the center of attention but *not* for the reason she assumed. Rather than admiring her hat, everyone was looking at a louse that first crawled on her clothes and then made its way to the top of her hat.

This story is told by Robert Burns (1759-96) in "To a Louse." I would have quoted it here verbatim except that it is written in an old Scottish dialect that is difficult to understand. Burns ended his poem with the following statement that is translated into contemporary English:

"Oh, would some Power give us the gift
To see ourselves as others see us!"

Thinking about my history teacher and the woman in the church, I have to ask myself: Would I *truly* want to know the way other people see me? In every possible circumstance?

What about you?

This is an uncomfortable thought because we know from personal observations that with some people, there is a huge gap between the way they see themselves in comparison to the way others see them.

People like this may try to inflate past accomplishments, flash money, or give advice on a wide variety of subjects. They kowtow to some individuals while treating others poorly. We usually feel a combination of revulsion and pity for people like this, and we may prefer to walk around the block to avoid even a brief conversation with them.

The spring 2008 semester culminated 22 years of my faculty service at Southern Methodist University. As a part of my finale there, I went to my classes one day wearing a diamond stud in my left earlobe. Then, when I rolled up the long sleeves on my shirt during the middle of lectures, students could see that I had a large tattoo of a shark on my right forearm. None of them said anything to me, but I could see them doing some double takes and whispering among themselves.

When I showed up two days later for the next session of those classes, I told them that April Fools' Day had come early. I didn't have a pierced ear, after all; the earring had been held on by a magnet. The shark tattoo was a fake, and I had washed it off.

After class was over, one young lady walked up and said that she had been disappointed in me. She was glad those things had been a joke. What she didn't need to say was the obvious: With my apparent pierced ear and tattoo, I was not being true to the person she knew me to be—I was acting like a phony.

My nephews, Peter and Andrew Sutherland, grew up in Colorado, and both turned into accomplished skiers and snowboarders. They have told me about people who show up at the slopes wearing all the right clothes and carrying all the right equipment but who don't know the first thing about gliding down the mountain. They're called posers.

There are posers in every facet of life, and they are easy to recognize by their actions.

On the other hand, we encounter individuals who pretty much know who they are. They don't have to put on airs; they don't try to impress and have no need to stretch the truth. They treat other people fairly, regardless of their position in society. We are much more apt to like these individuals and wish to associate with them.

Among the people with whom you are acquainted, there is undoubtedly a great deal of variation in the disparity between their self-perceptions and the way others perceive them. The greater the gap, the more out of touch the person is.

An enormous difference in this gap was discovered among some mental hospital patients studied by social psychologist Milton Rokeach in the early 1960s. Details of this research are found in his book, *The Three Christs of Ypsilanti*.[1] The title refers to Ypsilanti State Hospital in southeastern Michigan where Rokeach focused on three men, each deluded to the point where he claimed to be God.

These patients were in separate wards prior to the study, but Rokeach grouped them together in both living arrangements and other activities. Would this contact with others making the same claim lead them to relinquish their delusions of deity?

The answer was no, although one of them did seem to make temporary progress. From reading about these men, it is obvious that they were detached so far from reality, they had no idea about God's identity or their own. While each thought he was God, it was obvious to anyone even approaching normality that all three were insane.

Rokeach said these men had been diagnosed as schizophrenics. As such, there may have been genetic and other factors beyond their control that led to their seemingly unalterable conditions.

Despite this, they make a point for the majority of us who have the ability to make choices. People who play God are on a self-destructive course toward total spiritual blindness where the line between themselves and God becomes obscured completely. This has been the case with numerous dictators and mass murderers. At the same time, it probably is true of thousands of people who give appearances of being normal, yet they have the potential to inflict great harm on others. For instance, what is the spiritual state of a clergy member who tells himself it is okay to molest children?

Are such people insane, criminal, or both? They could be one or both, but those considerations are effects, and they are judged as such by societal standards. The cause is spiritual blindness, and this is judged by God.

What is pride?

When I was growing up, I don't recall hearing much, if anything, at church about how Satan might try to influence my life. I did hear that the devil was guilty of pride, and this subsequently played into my negative ideas about Christianity. Namely, you mean that Christians are not supposed to be proud of their accomplishments? That they should think everyone else is better than them and walk around with hang-dog expressions? That if I am miserable enough in this life, I could join other equally miserable people in Heaven?

Such ideas coincide with Satan's insinuation to Eve that God was holding something back from her.[2] This lie has been perpetuated in the millennia since then, and I bought into it.

What I didn't know was that pride is an unusual word because it has duel, nearly opposite meanings. Here are the definitions from the tattered pocket dictionary that has been my writing companion for the past 30-some years:

1. a) an overhigh opinion of oneself; b) haughtiness, arrogance
2. dignity and self-respect
3. satisfaction in something done, owned etc.
4. a person or thing in which pride is taken[3]

The basis for misunderstanding is clear. The first definition has a negative meaning, and it applies to Satan and any form of playing God. The rest of them have mostly positive connotations.

Both the positive and negative uses of pride may be found in the Bible.

In the positive sense, Paul's words in II Corinthians have been translated into English as follows: "I have great confidence in you; I take great *pride* in you."[4]

Elsewhere in II Corinthians, both meanings of pride are found in the same verse. "We are not trying to commend ourselves to you again, but are giving you an opportunity to take *pride* in us, so that you can answer those who take *pride* in what is seen rather than in what is in the heart."[5]

Thinking about the source of evil in terms of pride in the negative sense, is it possible for anyone to have any more haughtiness or arrogance or exhibit a higher opinion of self than Satan?

As an angel, Satan enjoyed a face-to-face relationship with God. He then decided that he could be God and led a revolution among the angels to overthrow the Almighty. He led humanity astray.

Satan's influence may be found behind every lie, injustice, and murder that ever has occurred on this earth.

Satan's "desire was to be *like* God, not to be unlike Him. Ironically, this arrogant desire would make him as much *unlike* God as it is possible to be!" according to author Erwin W. Lutzer.[6]

Putting these pieces together, we may conclude that Satan possesses the ultimate in pride in the negative sense.

Pride is an attitude that goes hand in hand with playing God. The Bible also links it to self-destruction.

"Pride goes before destruction, a haughty spirit before a fall."[7]

"The Lord detests all the proud of heart. Be sure of this: They will not go unpunished."[8]

"Haughty eyes and a proud heart, the lamp of the wicked, are sin!"[9]

In a prophecy about the country of Edom, a country whose inhabitants thought they could not be defeated because of their seemingly impregnable location in the clefts of a mountain, Jeremiah described the result of pride:

"The terror you inspire and the pride of your heart have deceived you."[10] As you can see, pride led these people into denial. The same thing occurs today.

The verse continues, "'Though you build your nest as high as the eagle's, from there I will bring you down,' declares the Lord."[11] This is another example of pride leading to self-destruction.

An important claim

Earlier, we made a link between insanity and claims to being the Almighty.

Jesus Christ said he was God.[12] What are we to conclude about this?

Either Jesus was telling the truth, or he was like one of the men in the mental hospital studied by Rokeach. There is no middle ground. We cannot say that Jesus was simply a wise man or a great leader. Even some atheists concede that Jesus was an extraordinary man.

The most important decisions of our lives boil down to these possibilities: Either Jesus Christ is God, or he is insane. Either Satan is God, or he is insane.

Which of the two will lead you in truth? Who is a liar?

Who will you follow?

Who will you serve?

Your answers operate not only to determine the overall direction of your life and the destination of your soul, but also to guide the many decisions you make each day.

True humility

Humility is another word that is misunderstood. Here's the way I define it: *Humility* means that a person understands his/her exact identity, knows who God is, and has a solid grasp of the gap between self and God.

During his earthly ministry, Jesus Christ comprehended the precise nature of his identity. He was the son of God, God in the flesh, and this means there was no gap.

John Eldridge observed, "When Christ is assaulted by the Evil One in the wilderness, the attack is ultimately on his identity. 'If you are the Son of God,' Satan sneers. . ., 'then prove it.'"[13] Jesus knew who He was and didn't have to prove anything to Satan.

By never wavering from his true identity, Jesus Christ exhibited the ultimate in *humility*.

Satan stands at the furthest extreme of pride.

Scriptures address these polar opposites:

"God opposes the proud but gives grace to the humble."[14]

"When pride comes, then comes disgrace, but with humility comes wisdom."[15] "The Lord sustains the humble but casts the wicked to the ground."[16]

"Before his downfall a man's heart is proud, but humility comes before honor."[17]

"The greatest among you will be your servant. For whoever exalts himself will be humbled, and whoever humbles himself will be exalted."[18]

Humility or humiliation?

Humility is a word often confused with humiliation. The words are related because both come from the same Latin base,[19] but in some ways, they are opposites.

Here's an illustration:

Considering my poor academic performance earlier in life, I was astounded that I earned a master's degree at Texas Tech University. Even more amazing to me was that I was asked to join the fulltime faculty at Texas Tech. I taught there for four years.

During that time, I came to see that if I really planned to continue teaching at the university level, I needed to earn a doctor's degree. Earlier in life, I never had given any thought to attaining this level of education; it was something that seemed simply beyond my reach.

I applied to Ph.D. programs at three universities, and lo and behold, all three accepted me. I started work toward my doctorate in the College of Communication at the University of Texas at Austin in the fall 1983. Around the same time, I had a book manuscript accepted by a major Christian publishing company, and it was due to be introduced in early 1984.

Reflecting on these things, I gave myself some pats on the back. I was going to be a doctor! I had written a book that probably would be an international best seller! Besides that, the book was being considered as a movie! If you think it sounds like me-me-me was in charge, you are correct.

At church my first Sunday after moving to Austin, several people introduced themselves. One of them was a white-haired man who stood about shoulder-high on me. (I'm close to 6 feet, two inches tall, so this is quite common.) Two seconds after he told me his name, I couldn't have repeated it. He then asked about me-me-me, and I went to great lengths to oblige him with plenty of information. Toward the end of my oration, I finally decided to ask about him. (I still cringe at the way I asked.) "By the way, what's your line?"

"I'm chief justice of the Texas Supreme Court."

For the record, his name is Jack Pope, and he wasn't kidding.

It suddenly hit me that I was standing there bragging about my pea-shooter when this man had the metaphorical equivalent of an arsenal that he never mentioned. I felt humiliated and walked away dumfounded (By the way, my pocket dictionary tells me this word may also be spelled dumbfounded.[20] That fits, too.)

Was it Justice Pope's wish for me to be humiliated? Certainly not. It was something I did to myself. If I had acted with a little bit of humility, I could have avoided it.

"Do not exalt yourself in the king's presence, and do not claim a place among great men; it is better for him to say to you, 'Come up here,' than for him to humiliate you before a nobleman."[21]

Jesus was humble and wants the same for us. Satan, the originator of pride, wants us to be humiliated.

For people who perceive God as cruel and punishing, it makes a great deal of sense that they think their god wants them to be humiliated. (Who or what is their god?)

As a postscript to this section, I thought you'd want to know about the outcomes of the earlier-mentioned expectations I had upon entering my doctoral program in 1983.

The book was published in 1984 but did not come close to being the best seller I had anticipated. The motion picture based on this story still has not been produced.

I did, however, earn a doctorate.

One day in December 1986, a large brown envelope came in the mail. It contained a suitable-for-framing document engraved with words indicating that I possessed a Ph.D. I stared at it for a few minutes, trying to grasp its significance. Then holding it between my thumb and forefinger, I sailed it across the room as if throwing a Frisbee. I then retrieved it and returned it to the envelope. A few months later, I took it out to show my parents, and to my best recollection, it has not left the envelope since that day.

My feelings about the Ph.D. were not unlike my sentiment after buying the used Corvette 17 years earlier. (For you Longhorn fans or Corvette drivers, these reactions had nothing to do with the degree-granting institution or the car but simply reflect the emptiness I always feel when trying to put anything but God into the God-shaped hole in my heart.)

It's personal

There is a big difference between the shaky soul who entered the mental hospital on the brink of suicide and the man I am today. (Before anyone else says it, I don't mean the graying hair and the growing bald spot on the back of my head.) Today, I may humiliate myself on occasions, but I don't go through each and every day as a humiliated individual as I did toward the end of my drinking.

The difference between then and now is strictly by the grace of God. I know that like the demon-possessed man described in Mark 5 who was on the fast track to self-destruction,[22] I had reached a point where no human being could help me. It was then that I sought my Savior and started on a journey toward Him. During all the years since, never once have I looked in the mirror and wondered who I was.

The Lord intervened on my behalf as he did with the demon-possessed man. That man, then in his right mind, wanted to accompany Jesus. Instead, he was told, "Go home to your family and tell them how much the Lord has done for you, and how he has had mercy on you."[23] Although the formerly demon-possessed man probably did tell his family, the Bible does not specify it, but it does say, "So the man went away and began to tell in the Decapolis how much Jesus had done for him. And all the people were amazed."[24] The Decapolis included 10 cities.[25]

For several years after I sobered up, I mostly kept my past a secret from people at church. Maybe there was a purpose for this in that it was a time for learning and growing. Finally, around 1980, I went on a weekend retreat with the singles' class from the church I attended in Lubbock, Texas. The minister asked me to prepare a talk to give during our Sunday morning worship service.

I got up in front of them all and told about my past as a drunk, how I had ended up in a mental hospital, and what the Lord had done for me. My fellow classmates were wide-eyed and opened-mouthed, and it marked the beginning of a new relationship with them. Little did I know, there were some people in that class who needed to hear that message. Several of them had snuck off the night before, visited a bar, and come back to the church camp half loaded.

I guess you could say that the Sunday morning lesson at the singles' retreat marked the beginning of my public ministry as a former drunkard. Since then, I've talked to thousands of people on the same subject. Like the formerly demon-possessed man, my message is what the Lord has done for me.

Now, I've shared my message with you, too.

If I remember the source of my strength and give Him the credit for every blessing, I am on a journey toward humility. Of course, the problem is that I easily get caught up in my pride of academic achievements and being an author not to mention judging, anger, resentments, fear, the list goes on and on.

Who am I, though, to take pride in anything? This is true insanity, because I know that if I had kept on drinking, I would not have reached age 30. My gratitude list, therefore, can start with the most basic thing I have today, my life. This also means that any positive thing in my life today is through grace.

Picture this: Suppose I wished to resume my academic career. At the very top of my academic vita, I write: "November 6, 1973; committed myself to a mental hospital for drunkenness." Do you think I would get a job? In God's hands, though, the worst day of my life has been turned into my greatest asset. When I get up to talk in front of a group, no one wants to hear about my academic success, but most people are interested in hearing what God has done with me.

Regarding his thorn in the flesh, Paul wrote, "Therefore I will boast all the more gladly about my weaknesses, so that Christ's power may rest on me."[26] The same thing is true for me, and I hope I remember this all day, every day for as long as the Lord grants me to be here.

A people magnet

Earlier, it was observed that people tend to like others who pretty much know who they are. This simply reflects that we are made in the image of God and that we innately recognize individuals who possess a measure of humility. This explains why Jesus Christ with 100% humility attracted a crowd wherever he went. It is not as though he was physically attractive[27] or that he was rich or aristocratic in the earthly sense. By his words and deeds, people were amazed[28] and recognized him as the real McCoy.

Jesus was not loved universally, however. His enemies were the religious experts of their day, and they looked at Jesus through the murky perspective of their me-me-me theology. They claimed to love God but didn't recognize Him when they met him face to face. We know these people had it backward because Jesus called them children of Satan.[29] His enemies were responsible for having him crucified, but in this act and his bodily resurrection that followed, Jesus defeated his chief enemy and ours.

What are the ramifications of this for us? Here is what Paul wrote:

> Your attitude should be the same as that of Christ Jesus:
> Who, being in very nature God,
> did not consider equality with God
> something to be grasped,
> but made himself nothing,
> taking the very nature of a servant,
> being made in human likeness.
> And being found in appearance as a man,
> he humbled himself
> and became obedient to death—
> even death on a cross!
> Therefore God exalted him to the highest place
> and gave him the name that is above every name,
> that at the name of Jesus every knee should bow,
> in heaven and on earth and under the earth,
> and every tongue confess that Jesus Christ is Lord,
> to the glory of God the Father.[30]

Who's doing the perceiving?

This chapter started with a history teacher and a woman in church who, at one particular time for each, did not know the way others saw them. We then identified a gap between what people think about themselves and what other people think about them. Now let's go a step further.

All people have biases that impact the way they see others; no human being is completely objective. As a result, we perceive the same situation somewhat differently.

God, on the other hand, looks at every situation with absolute objectivity. This means the infinitely more important question is not what other people think, *but what God thinks*. Our greatest concern, then, is the gap between the way we perceive ourselves and the way God perceives us.

What does God think about Jesus Christ? "This is my Son, whom I love; with him I am well pleased. Listen to him!"[31]

What does God think about Satan? I'm not going to venture to speculate about what God knows or thinks. We do know from the Bible, however, that Satan was cursed for deceiving humanity and was told that Jesus would crush his head[32] and that this was accomplished with the Lord's death, burial, and resurrection. Satan's destination is eternal torment in "the lake of burning sulfur."[33]

What does God think about us? After creating humanity "God

CHARTING THE DIFFERENCE

JESUS	SATAN
GOD IN THE FLESH AND KNEW IT	PLAYED GOD BUT IS JUST THE OPPOSITE
100% HUMILITY	0% HUMILITY
0% PRIDE	100% PRIDE
WANTS US TO HAVE HUMILITY	WANTS US TO BE HUMILIATED
LEADS OTHERS TO THE TRUTH	LEADS OTHERS IN A LIE
SPIRITUAL CLARITY	SPIRITUAL BLINDNESS
REALITY	UNREALITY
OFFERS ETERNAL LIFE	DESTINED FOR ETERNAL DEATH

saw all that he had made, and it was very good."[34] This is us! We also have the honor of being made in His image.[35] On top of this, God loved us so much that he sent his son to die for us.[36]

We will be on the road to humility if we remember that we are made in God's image and try to act accordingly. For our example, we look to the words and actions of Jesus as God in the flesh.

We will strive to reach a point where there is no gap between the way we see ourselves and the way God perceives us. That means we would have 100% humility and perfect spiritual vision, the very same as Jesus Christ.

Due to the murky vision of living in this fallen world, however, we will fall short of this goal. In the end, Jesus will make up the difference for us, enabling us to have the face-to-face relationship with our Creator that was enjoyed by Adam and Eve.

"We'll see it all then, see it all as clearly as God sees us, knowing him directly just as he knows us!"[37]

Endnotes: Chapter Twelve

1. Milton Rokeach, *The Three Christs of Ypsilanti*, Knopf, New York, NY, 1964.
2. Genesis 3:1, 5.
3. *Webster's New World Dictionary Revised Popular Library Pocket-Sized Edition*, The World Publishing Co., New York, 1973, p. 452.
4. II Corinthians 7: 4.
5. II Corinthians 5:12.
6. Erwin W. Lutzer, *The Serpent of Paradise: The Incredible Story of How Satan's Rebellion Serves God's Purposes*, Moody Press, Chicago, IL, 1996, p. 30.
7. Proverbs 16: 18.
8. Proverbs 16:5.
9. Proverbs 21: 4.
10. Jeremiah 49: 16.
11. Jeremiah 49: 16.
12. John 10:30; John 14: 10-11.
13. John Eldridge, *Wild at Heart: Discovering the Secret of a Man's Soul,* Thomas Nelson, Inc., Nashville, TN, 2001, p. 162; Luke 4: 1-13.
14. James 4:6.
15. Proverbs 11:2.
16. Psalm 147: 6.
17. Proverbs 18: 12.
18. Matthew 23: 11-12.
19. *Webster's New World Dictionary Revised Popular Library Pocket-Sized Edition,* op. cit., p. 281.
20. *Webster's New World Dictionary Revised Popular Library Pocket-Sized Edition,* op. cit., pp. 181-182.
21. Proverbs 25: 6-7.
22. Mark 5: 2-5.
23. Mark 5: 19.
24. Mark 5:20.
25. *The Family Worship Bible, New International Version*, Broadman and Holman Publishers, Nashville, TN, 1991, p.1059.
26. II Corinthians 12: 9.
27. Isaiah 53: 2.
28. Matthew 7: 28; 13: 54; Mark 1:22; 6:2; Luke 4:32; John 7: 46.
29. John 8: 42-47.
30. Philippians 2: 5-11.
31. Matthew 3: 17.
32. Genesis 3: 14-15.
33. Revelation 20:10.
34. Genesis 1: 31.
35. Genesis 1: 27.
36. John 3: 16.
37. I Corinthians 13: 12, *The Message.*

Questions for Self-Examination and Group Discussion: Chapter 12

1. This chapter discussed posers, individuals who seem to have one view of themselves while others around them see them completely differently. Without giving names, what are examples you've observed of posers in action? Why do posers not recognize themselves as posers? Is it possible that others view you as a poser but you don't know it?

2. How might someone in church get on a downward spiritual journey where the line between him/her and God eventually becomes completely blurred? Describe what might be going on in the mind of such an individual at various stages of this journey. What could occur in this person's life in order for him/her to change directions? What are some possible conclusions of this person's story?

3. How is the word "pride" misunderstood? You read about pride in the negative sense in relationship to Satan. How might this kind of pride manifest itself in someone who attends church every Sunday?

4. Tell why you agree or disagree with the author's premise in the following statement: "The most important decisions of our lives boil down to these possibilities: Either Jesus Christ is God, or he is insane. Either Satan is God, or he is insane."

5. After Jesus healed him, what was the greatest ministry tool of the formerly demon-possessed man discussed in Mark 5? What did the author say was his greatest ministry tool? What is yours?

6. How did Jesus Christ demonstrate 100% humility? How did Satan demonstrate 100% pride? Describe your ongoing battle between pride and humility.

7. When we leave our bodies at the end of this life, our murky vision will suddenly be gone, and we will have a face-to-face relationship with God. Describe the murky vision that you have today. Speculate as to the difference between your present vision and the one you will enjoy with God.

ACKNOWLEDGMENTS

The seeds for this book were planted with a question asked of me around 1990.

At the time, I was writing a book manuscript that would be published two years later, *Twelve Steps to a Closer Walk with God.* It describes the biblical origin of the 12 steps to recovery formulated by the program of Alcoholics Anonymous in the late 1930s that subsequently were adopted by some 200 other groups to address a wide variety of problems.

I wondered why an identical spiritual solution applied to such diverse addictions and finally came to the answer which served as a premise for that book: The steps take people from self-centered (no matter what the problem) to God-centered.

I had finished about six chapters of the manuscript and given them to Dr. John and Sandy Bell, friends at church. I went over to their house for feedback and sat down expecting a lot of pats on the back. Instead, I got a little praise and *the* question: Where does Satan fit into this picture?

I thought I had it nailed with my premise about being self-centered. Satan's role never had crossed my mind. Although I didn't think so at first, it was a great question, and one that would not go away.

Was it really possible that Satan had nothing to do with people killing themselves with addictions? Hardly. I did some additional research and added a couple of pages to the beginning of the 12-step book.

Even with that book published, I kept pondering John and Sandy's question.

In 1996, I was a member of the Singles II class at my home congregation, the Prestoncrest Church of Christ in Dallas, Texas. I was asked to teach for three months and planned to explain the biblical basis of the 12 steps, based on my earlier book. I did further research on Satan for the first session of the series, but that introductory material lasted for three weeks.

The following year, I taught the Singles II class again, this time devoting an entire quarter to the topic of how Satan attempts to influence our everyday lives.

In the decade or so since then, I've taught this series to many of the Sunday morning adult classes at our church. Due to questions and observations of the people who attended those sessions, the material continually took on greater depth and breadth. Finally, they started encouraging me to put the material into book form.

I began work on the manuscript in 2006.

My mother, Mary Evelyn Umphrey, and sister, Jan Sutherland, both read early drafts. Kim, whom I met at church in 1999 and married in 2001, has given me continual feedback. Others reading the final draft besides my wife were Steve Steele, Bill Beeman, and Steven C. Phillips.

I'm also very grateful for the considerable guidance I received from my literary agent, Les Stobbe, and also to Kimberly Shumate, an editor at Harvest House Publishers, who confirmed that this material was not only publishable but much needed. I hope you agree with that assessment.

Don Umphrey, October 2008

Notes

Notes

NOTES

Notes